MW01256643

A Cluster of Camphire

Words of Cheer and Comfort for Sick and Sorrowful Souls!

BY

Mrs. C. H. Spurgeon

1898

(Written by Susannah Spurgeon after the death
of her beloved husband Charles Spurgeon)

Edited by

Teresa Suttles

ISBN:9781543270914

Camphire: a flowering shrub having clusters of fragrant, cream-colored flowers that were highly valued in ancient times

Song of Solomon 1:14: *My beloved is unto me as a cluster of camphire in the vineyards of Engedi.*

Other Books by this Author

The Little Gray Box

John Bunyan's The Holy War: An Updated Edition

The Life of John Bunyan — Christian Biography Series

Thongzai Mamma: The Life of Marilla Baker Ingalls — Christian Biography Series

Under the Hopia Tree: The Life of Ann Judson — Christian Biography Series

Gentle and Quiet Strength: 6 Ladies, 5 Brilliant Hymnwriters – Christian Biography Series

The Mighty Side of Weaker – Christian Biography Series

Pillars of Piety and Poison – Christian Biography Series

Rev. John Hill Sermons Edited by this Author
It is Well: Faith's Estimate of Afflictive Dispensations
The Sinfulness of Sin: Sermons on Repentance and Regeneration
Christ the Best of Blessings
For the Comfort of the Saints

Mrs. C. H. Spurgeon Books Edited by this Author
A Basket of Summer Fruit
A Cluster of Camphire
A Carillon of Bells

FORWARD

True love merits its reward, it does not seek it—so wrote Bernard of Clairvaux (1090-1153). What an apt description of a woman who so completely devoted her adult life to the service of her Lord that not even the confinement to her sickbed could deter her from her work. Never was her obedience impeded by her pain, and her life continues to testify of her love for Christ. This was Susannah Spurgeon.

Three delightful books were written by Mrs. Spurgeon after the death of her beloved husband Charles Haddon Spurgeon in 1892. *A Basket of Summer Fruit*, *A Carillon of Bells*, and *A Cluster of Camphire* provide devotional thoughts on texts of Scripture that address various times and trials in the lives of all Christians. These very personal reminiscences of Mr. Spurgeon's dear Susie contemplate the timeless truths of Scriptures that can be readily applied to every Christian in every age.

But old copies of the early printings are rarely available. That is why we have committed to the reprinting of all three books. In preparing the text written by Susannah Spurgeon herself, we became convinced that readers of these books today may be benefited in a richer way by the addition of some definitions, explanations, and Scripture references added as footnotes. These footnotes are not intended to be a distraction from Mrs. Spurgeon's rich writing; they are simply meant to be an aid for a clearer understanding and a further blessing in Christian study. Once readers meet her, they will be persuaded that all these loving embellishments would have Susannah's approval!

By including a biography of this pious Christian lady, we hope to provide readers a peek behind the curtain of the author's name to see the very writer herself and a bit of what shaped and molded her in her Christian life. But we would be remiss if we failed to confess another motive—to inspire women, young and old, to love the Lord Jesus Christ with their whole hearts. It will be their abiding, unswerving love for Him that will motivate their sacrificial service to Him. Then they, too, shall be known in years to come just as Susannah Spurgeon continues to be known—by her fruits.

Teresa Suttles
2017

For every tree is known by his own fruit.
Luke 6:44

.

MRS. C. H. SPURGEON

Treasured up within the petals resides the fragrance of the rose. Lovely though the rose is to gaze upon, the vision of its beauty too soon fades. Only the pungent sweetness of its fragrance will linger. But that, too, will last but a moment unless its glorious potency is captured. Then its fragrance will endure to captivate those who never saw the beauty of the rose nor realized that the memory existed of such a beauty. It will be that fragrance, captured while the beauty of the rose still dazzled the eye of the beholder, that is released to soothe the generations not yet born.

Many roses bloom, but the fragrance of only a few will endure. For the perfume of the fragrance can only be made by the bruising of the rose. The petals of those chosen roses first must be gathered, then pressed and broken into the oil. The fragrance of those broken petals learns to ride upon the carrier oil and to be delightfully effused in the work of the oil. So it was with the life of Susannah Spurgeon.

Mrs. Charles Haddon Spurgeon was born Susannah Thompson on January 15, 1832. Her parents, with their young daughter, often visited the services of the New Park Street Chapel, Southwark, in the southern district of London. The young Susannah would often visit her relatives Mr. and Mrs. Olney, an elderly couple in Southwark, and remain with them to attend their services in the Chapel.

It was on the Sunday evening of December 18, 1853, while attending service with Mr. and Mrs. Olney, that Susannah first saw the young preacher Charles H. Spurgeon as he filled the pulpit for that Lord's Day services.

Mr. Spurgeon soon accepted the pastorate of the Chapel, and Susannah often conversed with him in the Olney home. As she continued under the preaching of Mr. Spurgeon, Susannah was pricked with the conviction of her own spiritual coldness and lack of Christian service. She confided in her cousin William, the Olney son and a faithful worker in the Chapel Sunday School. He may have shared Susannah's concerns with the young pastor; but whatever served as the impetus, Mr. Spurgeon sent Susannah a copy of *The Pilgrim's Progress* inscribed with his desires "for her progress in the blessed pilgrimage."[i]

As the summer days of 1854 began to wane, Susannah Thompson and Charles Spurgeon announced their wedding engagement. Before the young couple married in January 1856, Susannah had already had ample opportunities to prepare herself for becoming a pastor's wife. Often the young bridegroom would break from his busy schedule to visit his bride-to-be carrying with him proofs of his sermons to revise for the printer. Rather than finding his attentiveness to his work offensive, she wrote: "'I learned to be quiet and to mind my own business while this important work was going on. It was good discipline for the Pastor's intended wife.'"[ii]

Twin baby boys enlarged their household in September 1856, providing boundless joy for the young couple. After the birth of her babies, Susannah testified that her "whole time and strength were given to advance my dear husband's welfare and happiness." She wrote: "I deemed it my joy and privilege to be ever at his side…"[iii]

With joyful enthusiasm, she managed the modest means of her household to be able to give financial assistance to young men seeking an education in preparation for the ministry. At times, it seemed almost impossible to "make ends meet"; yet her own willing effort helped in the organization of her husband's

Pastor's College. She wrote, "I rejoice to remember how I shared my beloved's joy when he founded the Institution, and that together we planned and pinched in order to carry out the purpose of his loving heart..."[iv]

The growth of the church congregation had precipitated an expansion of the old building, but soon it was outgrown completely. A new building was erected at Elephant and Castle in South London, completed in 1861 and with the new name Metropolitan Tabernacle.

For those first ten years as Mrs. Charles Spurgeon, Susannah recorded her "heartfelt gratitude to God...that I was permitted to encircle [her husband] with all the comforting care and tender affection which it was in a wife's power to bestow."[v]

But, at last, the day had come for the lovely rose to be pressed in a time of physical affliction and suffering. She wrote, in 1868, that her "travelling days were done" and "henceforth for many years I was a prisoner in a sick-chamber..."[vi] Her long times of confinement did not interfere with her faithful training of her sons. By their own testimony, both young Charles and Thomas traced their conversions as boys to the teaching and example of their godly mother; and neither would her sick chamber rob her of other service to her Lord.

In 1875, Mr. Spurgeon had completed his first volume of *Lectures to My Students*; and it was received by his dear Susie with the lament, "I wish I could place it in the hands of every minister in England."[vii] The early days of her management with a meager household budget proved to be the foundation of her sympathy for faithful pastors too poor to purchase theology books for their study and Christian growth. So when she voiced her desire to provide ministers with the new book, her husband issued a challenge: "How much will you give?"

Susannah's mind immediately began to calculate what part of her household funds could be used. But her memory lighted on a small hoard of coins she had stashed away through the years. When she calculated the sum, she had just enough to pay for one hundred copies of the new book. This was the inauguration of her Book Fund.

An 1875 advertisement in Mr. Spurgeon's periodical *The Sword and the Trowel*, invited poor Baptist ministers to apply for his book through Mrs. Spurgeon's fund. Not only did applications for the book flood in, but contributions poured in to assist in payment for an ever-increasing number of different books to be provided to those poor ministers without charge.

Mrs. Spurgeon's Book Fund grew exponentially, soon to be joined by the Pastors' Aid Fund. This second enterprise was begun when Mrs. Spurgeon was given a sum of money to assist poor pastors with the daily needs of their families.

Books were packaged, letters written, and finances were managed for these funds from Susannah's sickroom. The work was never hindered by her illness, and her diary entries from these days of pain do not reveal any rebellious or despairing spirit against such a Providence that required the continued crushing and bruising. Her biographer Charles Ray wrote:

> It is truly wonderful that being so often prostrated, Mrs. Spurgeon was able to keep the Book Fund in so flourishing a condition. Over and over again she was completely laid aside, and when once more convalescent her weakness was such that none but a woman whose whole being was given up to service for the Lord could have sustained the mental and physical stress

of such a great work.[viii]

Her beloved husband wrote of her:

I gratefully adore the goodness of our Heavenly Father in directing my beloved wife to a work which has been, to her, fruitful in unutterable happiness. That it has cost her more pain than it would be fitting to reveal is most true; but that it has brought her a boundless joy is equally certain.

Our gracious Lord ministered to His suffering child in the most effectual manner when He graciously led her to minister to the necessities of His servants.

Let every believer accept this as the inference of experience: that for most human maladies the best relief and antidote will be found in self-sacrificing work for the Lord Jesus.[ix]

In the later years of their marriage, Mrs. Spurgeon would often be separated for periods of time from her beloved husband when he would travel to France for the benefit of his own failing health. These times of forced separation were happily punctuated by letters of affectionate correspondence; and she described these separations as "very painful to hearts so tenderly united as were ours, but we each bore our share of the sorrow as heroically as we could and softened it as far as possible by constant correspondence."[x]

After several weeks in France, Mr. Spurgeon returned to his pulpit in the Tabernacle to preach one last time on the Lord's Day morning, June 7, 1891. His health seemed to worsen; but he rallied enough in October to return to France, accompanied by Susannah.

Sadly, Mr. Spurgeon was confined to bed on January 20, 1892. A few days later, he slipped into unconsciousness and passed away on January 31. Mrs. Spurgeon and a few of their friends knelt in prayer by the bed of her departed beloved. She then cabled her son Thomas: "Father in Heaven. Mother resigned."[xi]

In the dozen years that followed her husband's death, Mrs. Spurgeon spent her widowhood continuing her work in both the Book Fund and Pastors' Aid Fund. During these years, she also continued her writing, devoting much time to the compilation of Mr. Spurgeon's diary and letters into the four-volume *C. H. Spurgeon's Autobiography*. These were the years she also wrote the three, small devotional books—*A Carillon of Bells to Ring Out the Old Truths of 'Free Grace and Dying*

Love', A Cluster of Camphire or Words of Cheer and Comfort for Sick and Sorrowful Souls, and *A Basket of Summer Fruit*.

Susannah was confined to her bed, one last time, this time with pneumonia, in the summer of 1903. For weeks, she lingered; but at last, not long before leaving this world, she pressed together her feeble hands, uttering: "Blessed Jesus! Blessed Jesus! I can see the King in His Glory!"[xii]   Peacefully, she departed the confinement of this world on the morning of October 22, leaving her fragrance to linger for generations.

T. S.

---

[i] Charles Ray, *Mrs. C. H.* Spurgeon, (Pasadena: Pilgrim Publications, 1979), 11. This biography was first published in November, 1903.
[ii] Ibid., 27.
[iii] Ibid., 47-48.
[iv] Ibid., 35.
[v] Ibid., 48.
[vi] Ibid., 51.
[vii] Ibid., 67.
[viii] Ibid., 93.
[ix] Ibid., 93-94.
[x] Ibid., 51.
[xi] Ibid., 109.
[xii] Ibid., 117.

CONTENTS

SOUL-COMFORT

"In the multitude of my thoughts within me thy comforts delight my soul." Psalm 94:19

"Thy comforts delight any soul." Blessed Lord, how sweet is this text in my mouth! The taste of it is "like wafers made with honey."[1] It is both food and drink to my heart, for every word has joy and refreshing in it; so that, like the "best wine" of the Canticles, it "goes down sweetly, causing the lips of those who are asleep to speak."[2] "Thy comforts—Thy comforts delight my soul."[3]

Give me grace, dear Master, to sit at Your table, this morning, and eat and drink abundantly, as Your beloved ones may do, of the Divine dainties Your love has here provided! Help me so to speak of them, that not only my own soul—but the souls of others

_____

[1] Exodus 16:31: *And the house of Israel called the name thereof Manna: and it was like coriander seed, white; and the taste of it was like wafers made with honey.*
[2] Song of Solomon 7:9: *And the roof of thy mouth like the best wine for my beloved, that goeth down sweetly, causing the lips of those that are asleep to speak.*
[3] Psalm 94:19: *In the multitude of my thoughts within me thy comforts delight my soul.*

may enjoy the heavenly manna, and be filled with the mingled and spiced wine of remembrance and expectation![4] Human comforters we may have had, and we blessed them for their kindness; but none can comfort like You, for You are "the Father of mercies, and the God of all comfort."[5] Come then, dear Lord, help us to spread out this feast of fat things, and set it in order before our eyes, that we may see what reason we have to "comfort those who are in any trouble, by the comfort with which we ourselves are comforted of God."[6]

"When my anxious thoughts multiply within me," the first of Your comforts, gracious God, is this—that You have said unto my soul, "I am thy salvation!"[7] He saves us, not because of any merit in us, or any deservings of our

---

[4] Song of Solomon 8:2: *I would lead thee, and bring thee into my mother's house, who would instruct me: I would cause thee to drink of spiced wine of the juice of my pomegranate.*

[5] II Corinthians 1:3: *Blessed be God, even the Father of our Lord Jesus Christ, the Father of mercies, and the God of all comfort…*

[6] II Corinthians 1:4: *Who comforteth us in all our tribulation, that we may be able to comfort them which are in any trouble, by the comfort wherewith we ourselves are comforted of God.*

[7] Psalm 35:3: *Draw out also the spear, and stop the way against them that persecute me: say unto my soul, I am thy salvation.*

own; but because sovereign grace chose us, and Divine compassion redeemed us; and when we were far off, infinite pity brought us back, and made us near by the precious blood of Christ. It may well "comfort our hearts"— this "everlasting consolation and good hope through grace"[8]—coming as it does direct from "our Lord Jesus Christ Himself, and God, even our Father, who has loved us." A saved and pardoned sinner can truly say, "Your comforts delight my soul!"

The next thought is that, having saved us, He keeps us. "We are kept by the power of God through faith unto salvation."[9] Comparatively few Christians put God's keeping power fully to the test. If we would trust Him for the keeping, as we do for the saving—our lives would be far holier and happier than they are. "I will keep it every moment,"[10] is one of those grandly unlimited promises which most of us are afraid of; and we store them away in the

---

[8] II Thessalonians 2:16-17: *Now our Lord Jesus Christ himself, and God, even our Father, which hath loved us, and hath given us everlasting consolation and good hope through grace, Comfort your hearts, and stablish you in every good word and work.*

[9] I Peter 1:5: *Who are kept by the power of God through faith unto salvation ready to be revealed in the last time.*

[10] Isaiah 27:3: *I the Lord do keep it; I will water it every moment: lest any hurt it, I will keep it night and day.*

background because we dare not believe them, and bring them out into the light of our daily practice. O foolish and unbelieving hearts, how much of soul-delighting comfort do we thus miss!

Then comes another thought, He cares for us. Dear friends, if you are His, you know the exceeding comfort of casting all your care upon Him,[11] and being quite sure that He will "undertake" for you. Have we not often come to Him oppressed and burdened with an intolerable weight of anxiety and distress—and been enabled to roll the whole mass of it on Him, leaving it all at His feet, and returning to our work with a lightened and restful heart? Some of us have had burdens and sorrows, which would have crushed the very life out of us—if we had not been enabled to look up and say, "Thou, Lord, have helped and comforted me."[12] Yes, truly, God's care for us is one of the sweetest comforts of our mortal life!

Closely linked with this is that other thought, that He knows all about us. Our enemies—sometimes, even our friends—

---

[11] I Peter 5:7: *Casting all your care upon him; for he careth for you.*

[12] Psalm 86:17: *Shew me a token for good; that they which hate me may see it, and be ashamed: because thou, Lord, hast holpen me, and comforted me.*

misunderstand and malign[13] us; they misconstrue[14] our words and actions, and impute to us motives which never actuated[15] us. But our God knows the thoughts and intents of our heart, and never makes a mistake in the judgment He passes on us.[16] The comfort of this knowledge on the Lord's part, to those who are "suffering wrongfully,"[17] is inexpressibly precious. They can lift up their heads with joy, and say, "The Lord is good. He knows those who trust in Him."[18] I have known this comfort so delight my soul, that trials and temptations had no power to vex or annoy it, for it was hidden "secretly in a pavilion from the strife of tongues."[19]

---

[13] To speak harmful falsehoods, to slander, to smear
[14] Misunderstand
[15] To motivate, to activate, to set in motion to action
[16] Jeremiah 17:10: *I the Lord search the heart, I try the reins, even to give every man according to his ways, and according to the fruit of his doings.* Hebrews 4:12: *For the word of God is quick, and powerful, and sharper than any twoedged sword, piercing even to the dividing asunder of soul and spirit, and of the joints and marrow, and is a discerner of the thoughts and intents of the heart.*
[17] I Peter 2:19: *For this is thankworthy, if a man for conscience toward God endure grief, suffering wrongfully...*
[18] Nahum 1:7: *The Lord is good, a strong hold in the day of trouble; and he knoweth them that trust in him.*
[19] Psalm 31:20: *Thou shalt hide them in the secret of thy presence from the pride of man: thou shalt keep them secretly in a pavilion from the strife of tongues.*

Lastly (though there are many, many more), one of the multitude of thoughts which stand out prominently from the rest, as a comfort that delights the soul, is that He loves us. This truth has been running through the fields of previous thought, as a silver streamlet glides through the meadows—here, it should deepen and expand to a broad and fathomless ocean, had I the power to speak of its height, and depth, and length, and breadth, and to tell of the love of Christ, which surpasses knowledge.[20]

But my pen utterly fails here. I feel as John Berridge must have felt when he wrote, "We must die, to speak fully of Christ."[21] You who love Him, and know that He loves you—must each one say to himself what that "comfort of love" is to your own heart. This will be a better comment than any I can offer. And, if some poor distressed soul is mourning the loss of the

---

[20] Ephesians 3:17-19: *That Christ may dwell in your hearts by faith; that ye, being rooted and grounded in love, May be able to comprehend with all saints what is the breadth, and length, and depth, and height; And to know the love of Christ, which passeth knowledge, that ye might be filled with all the fullness of God.*

[21] John Berridge (1716-1793), English evangelist and hymn writer—*Vex'd I try and try again, Still my effort all are vain: Living tongues are dumb at best, We must die to speak of Christ.*

sweet consolation which Christ's love alone can give—let him call to remembrance a tenderly precious promise which the Lord put into the lips of the prophet Isaiah, *"I have seen his ways, and will heal him; I will lead him also, and restore comforts unto him."* Isaiah 57:18

A Wide-open Gate

*"The LORD taketh pleasure in them that fear Him,
in those that hope in His mercy."*
Psalm 147:11

It seems to me, that very many of the Lord's people are like timid sheep that stand trembling outside the fold, lingering by the fences, hungry and thirsty for the green pastures and still waters within the enclosure, but not daring to venture in. They are in the King's meadow, He has given His life for them, and called them by name; but something hinders their full enjoyment of His love, and of the dainties which that love has provided for them. They "cannot enter in because of unbelief,"[1] they are afraid to draw any nearer because they do not possess the "full assurance of faith."[2]

Poor, distressed, faint-hearted ones! This is not the will of God concerning you, nor is it the mind of your loving Shepherd, for He says,

---

[1] Hebrews 3:19: *So we see that they could not enter in because of unbelief.*

[2] Hebrews 10:22: *Let us draw near with a true heart in full assurance of faith, having our hearts sprinkled from an evil conscience, and our bodies washed with pure water.*

"My sheep hear My voice, and they follow Me";³ and following Christ always means getting closer to God, and learning to delight in Him.

This text is a wide-open gate into the fair fields of peace and joy, where you may find rest unto your souls. You need not stay to wonder whether you can ever get through; the way is plain and smooth, all the stones are gathered out; and if you will, you may come and be welcomed.

Did you not, just lately, see one quite as timorous⁴ as yourself go up to "the Man at the Gate," and ask for entrance? And do you not know what the ready reply was? "'I am willing with all My heart,' said He."⁵

And if you will venture, you will receive the same loving answer.

Let us look well at the blessed, encouraging words. "The Lord takes pleasure in those who fear Him." Can you not come in there? Do you not fear Him—I mean, in a

---

³ John 10:27-28: *My sheep hear my voice, and I know them, and they follow me: And I give unto them eternal life; and they shall never perish, neither shall any man pluck them out of my hand.*

⁴ Fearful

⁵ From John Bunyan's *The Pilgrim's Progress*: Goodwill opens the gate for Christian at the Wicket-gate

spiritual, not a slavish sense—fear to grieve Him, fear to go contrary to His will, fear to miss His approval, or occasion the hiding of His face? Then, if this is true, He takes pleasure in you! Think of it quietly for a moment. Lay down this little book, and let the precious hope steal into your heart, that this is truly message of comfort for you, and that it ought to be immediately received, believed, and rejoiced in.

Do not put it away from you, and refuse to accept the blessing because it seems "too good to be true," and you feel too sinful, too selfish, too half-hearted to be worthy of such tender love.

Besides, do you not see that, as if this gate were not open enough for such timid ones as you, "the Shepherd of Love" has flung it even further back in the next clause of the verse, "The Lord taketh pleasure in those that hope in His mercy." Surely, the most desponding[6] and fearful of the Lord's children can come as far as that, and with a lightened heart thankfully say, "Dear Lord, that must mean me!"

My friend, if you do, indeed, "fear the Lord, and hope in His mercy," you know it is not a question of what you are, but of what

[6] Despair, discouragement, hopelessness

Christ is for you. Faith in the Lord Jesus, strips
the soul of its filthy rags, and wraps around it
the glorious and priceless robe of the Savior's
righteousness; and thus arrayed, it is easy to
see that all who believe must be pleasing in the
Father's sight. Dear Mr. Spurgeon was very
fond of quoting two quaint lines which set
forth this reassuring truth—

> "Him, and then the sinner see,
> Look through Jesus' wounds on me."

Herein lies the secret of God's delight in
His people, and it is because we are "justified
freely by His grace, through the redemption
that is in Christ Jesus,"[7] that we dare to believe
that "the Lord is well pleased for His
righteousness' sake."[8] What a pity it is that we
often persist in looking more at our own
spiritual condition—than at Him who alone
can make that condition one of constant
abiding in Him! Miss Havergal[9], in her

---

[7] Romans 3:24: *Being justified freely by his grace through the
redemption that is in Christ Jesus.*
[8] Isaiah 42:21: *The Lord is well pleased for his righteousness'
sake; he will magnify the law, and make it honourable.*
[9] Frances Ridley Havergal (1836-1879), English hymn writer.
"Take my Life and Let It Be" and "Like a River Glorious" are
two of her well-known hymns

delightful little book, "My King," very strikingly says: "Let us leave off morbidly looking to see exactly how much we love Him, for this is like trying to warm ourselves at a thermometer, and perhaps only ends in doubting whether we love Him at all!"

Ah! dear souls, a far better way is to believe God's Word, and joyfully think of Him as taking pleasure in you, rejoicing in your desire after Him, and the hope in His mercy which He sees in your heart.

Remember that the "fear "and the "hope" are His own work in you, they are not the natural products of your soul, but spiritual graces implanted by the Holy Spirit. Take courage, then, get a grip of the blessed truth that He loves you—He loves you—and, soon, instead of wandering forlornly[10] up and down the outside pastures, you will be drawn by that love to the inner fold where "He feeds among the lilies."[11]

––––––––––––––––––––––––––––

[10] Miserable, unhappy

[11] Song of Solomon 2:16: *My beloved is mine, and I am his: he feedeth among the lilies.*

Tables in the Wilderness

"Can God furnish a table in the wilderness?"
Psalm 78:19

To be sure He can! The question is a most distrustful and cruel one! Our indignation burns against the rebellious people who could thus discredit the power of their gracious God, though He had done such great things for them. "He clave the rocks in the wilderness, and gave them drink, as out of the great depths. He brought streams also out of the rock, and caused waters to run down like rivers."[1] He had delivered them from galling bonds of slavery, and had fed them with bread from Heaven; yet they doubted His ability to supply them with the food their heart desired, and "they spoke against God "[2] in thus questioning His love and care.

As we read their history, and wonder at their hardness of heart, we say, "How could they be so blind, so ungrateful, so perversely

---

[1] Psalm 78:15: *He clave the rocks in the wilderness, and gave them drink as out of the great depths.*

[2] Psalm 78:19: *Yea, they spake against God; they said, Can God furnish a table in the wilderness?*

unbelieving?" But, the next moment, we bow our heads in shame, and our own hearts condemn us as we remember how often we have committed the very same sin. We, too, have "limited the Holy One of Israel,"[3] and grieved the Spirit of our gracious God by our persistent unbelief; for, many a time have we thought, even if we have not said it, "Can God furnish a table in the wilderness?"[4] when His loving, bounteous hand has been preparing and spreading it before us!

Have you not found it so? Have you not sometimes been shamed into a lively[5] faith, by receiving the very blessings which you doubted the Lord's power to give? Has He not often proved Himself "able to do exceeding abundantly above all that you have asked or thought,"[6] even while your faithless heart has "believed not in God, and trusted not in His salvation"?[7]

_____

[3] Psalm 78:41: *Yea, they turned back and tempted God, and limited the Holy One of Israel.*

[4] Psalm 78:19

[5] Active, living

[6] Ephesians 3:20-21: *Now unto him that is able to do exceeding abundantly above all that we ask or think, according to the power that worketh in us, Unto him be glory in the church by Christ Jesus throughout all ages, world without end. Amen.*

[7] Psalm 78:22: *Because they believe not in God, and trusted*

Dear readers, I would gladly take you into the wilderness with me this morning, and bid you look back upon some of the "tables" which, in past days, the Lord has furnished for you there.

Do you not remember that desert experience of sore affliction, when you were laid very low, when heart and flesh failed, and you were brought into the dust of death? Did not the Lord then come and strengthen you upon "the bed of languishing,"[8] and tenderly furnish your sick-room table with the rich cordials of His love, and the life-giving elixir[9] of His healing power? And, after that display of His mercy—can you not recollect how quickly the fever left you, and what joy it was to rise and minister unto Him?[10]

Or—have you forgotten that dread hour of spiritual darkness, a "waste howling

---

not in his salvation...

[8] Psalm 41:3: *The LORD will strengthen him upon the bed of languishing: thou wilt make all his bed in his sickness.*

[9] Cordial: a sweetened drink or a medicine that gives energy and feeling of well-being/Elixir: a sweet substance, usually in liquid form that is used in medicines; can refer to "magical potions"; a remedy

[10] Mark 1:31: *And he came and took her by the hand, and lifted her up; and immediately the fever left her, and she ministered unto them.*

wilderness"[11] of terror, when your soul was assailed by some horrible temptation, and Satan beset you so furiously that, for a moment, you almost despaired of deliverance? Was not that very moment the time of the Lord's gracious relief and succour?[12] Did He not appear on your behalf, and lead you forth from the conflict, to find the table of His love spread as for a banquet for your sake, and the leaves of the Tree of Life ready plucked for the healing of your wounds?

Can you not recall those other seasons of distress, when some sad bereavement, or some great crisis of your life had brought you into a Sahara of desolation and grief? Almost broken in heart, your soul fainted within you, and you "wandered in the wilderness in a solitary way,"[13] believing yourself to be cut off from the land of the living. But you cried unto God; and how blessedly did He answer you! He turned the dry ground into water-springs, the sandy desert into a rich pasturage of grace and mercy, and there He prepared "a table before

---

[11] Deuteronomy 32:10: *He found him in a desert land, and in the waste howling wilderness; he led him about, he instructed him, he kept him as the apple of his eye.*

[12] Comfort, help, aid, assistance

[13] Psalm 107:4: *They wandered in the wilderness in a solitary way; they found no city to dwell in.*

you," and the desert yielded royal dainties!

Ah! these tables in the wilderness! They are standing rebukes to our lack of faith, and constant memorials of God's faithfulness and love! Yes, but times without number it is true of us, as of those cities we read of in the Gospels, where "He did not many mighty works there, because of their unbelief."[14] God does not work wonders for us if we mistrust Him; His miracles of grace and power, are wrought on behalf of those whose faith is strong enough to claim the performance of His Word. How very few of us, who call ourselves Christians, ever live up to our high privileges, as "heirs of God, and joint-heirs with Christ"![15] Did we but realize our true position as sons and daughters of the Lord God Almighty, there would be nothing impossible to us.

A recent writer on this subject says: "If there is a discrepancy[16] between our life and the fulfillment and enjoyment of all God's promises—the fault is ours. If our experience is

---

[14] Matthew 13:58: *And he did not many mighty works there because of their unbelief.*

[15] Romans 8:16-17: *The Spirit itself beareth witness with our spirit, that we are the children of God: And if children, then heirs; heirs of God, and joint-heirs with Christ; if so be that we suffer with him that we may be also glorified together.*

[16] Difference, disagreement

not what God wants it to be—it is because of our unbelief in the love of God, in the power of God, and in the reality of His promises."[17]

Is not this the reason why so many of God's own children are living at such a miserably low level of spiritual existence? It is a positive fact that they do not believe what God has said. They are as distrustful as if He had never given them the blessed assurance, "I am the Lord, I do not change";[18] as poor as though He had never made the promise, "Whatsoever ye shall ask in My name, that will I do";[19] and as unhappy and full of worry as if His own lips had not spoken those other sweet words, "Let not your heart be troubled: ye believe in God, believe also in Me."[20]

Beloved, when you think of the wilderness through which you have already been brought, never forget the tables and their furnishings which were there prepared for you. This will help you to trust God for the future, while you praise Him for the past!

---

[17] Andrew Murray, *The Deeper Christian Life: An Aid to Its Attainment*, circa 1895.
[18] Malachi 3:6: *For I am the LORD, I change not; therefore ye sons of Jacob are not consumed.*
[19] John 14:13: *And whatsoever ye shall ask in my name, that will I do, that the Father may be glorified in the Son.*
[20] John 14:1

A Prisoner's Brave Faith

"There is nothing too hard for Thee."
Jeremiah 32:17

Shut up in a prison in Jerusalem—the city about to be besieged, and its inhabitants threatened with captivity—the prophet is yet commanded to buy a field, observing all the customary forms of purchase, just as if matters were not at such an awful crisis. The Lord's servant obeys at once; without question or delay; he purchases the field, and weighs out the money, with apparently no chance of ever seeing or rejoicing in his possession. Splendid faith this! And we see the secret springs of his confidence when he exultingly says, "Ah, Lord God! Behold, You have made the heavens and the earth by Your great power and outstretched arm, *there is nothing too hard for Thee.*"

It is worthy of note that these words so pleased the Lord that, further on in the chapter, He takes them into His own lips, and repeats them to the prophet, asking, *Is anything too hard for Me?*

Dear reader, your difficulties and trials

may not be comparable or similar to those of "the weeping prophet,"[1] but they are very real, and seemingly insurmountable to you; and it is a fact that, of yourself, you can neither overcome nor endure them, so I want to remind you that the Lord's hand is not shortened[2]—that what was true of His power in Jeremiah's time, is as certainly true today— and that whatever present hardship may press upon you, or whatever burden may be weighing you down—you, yes, you may look up to Him with confident faith, and say, "There is nothing too hard for Thee."[3]

Oh, the blessed peace which such an assurance brings! I do not know what your particular sorrow or hardship may be—but I do know that, whatever its nature—cruel, or bitter, or hopeless—it is as "nothing" to Him! He is able to deliver you as easily as you can call upon Him for support and help.

Now, dear friend, think of all the hard

---

[1] Jeremiah is known as the "weeping prophet." Lamentations 3:48-50: *Mine eye runneth down with rivers of water for the destruction of the daughter of my people. Mine eye trickleth down, and ceaseth not, without any intermission, Till the LORD look down, and behold from heaven.*

[2] Isaiah 59:1: *Behold, the LORD'S hand is not shortened, that it cannot save; neither his ear heavy, that it cannot hear…*

[3] Jeremiah 32:27: *Behold, I am the LORD, the God of all flesh: is there any thing too hard for me?*

things there are in your life—hard circumstances, difficult duties, grievous pains, sore struggles, bitter disappointments, hard words, hard thoughts, a hard heart of your own, a hard heart in others—gather all these, and many more together, and pile them one on another till you have one great mountain of adamant[4]—your God still calmly asks the question, "Is there anything too hard for Me?"

When our hearts are weary of life's cares and crosses, when our courage flags[5] because of our helplessness, and we cry out with the patriarch, "All these things are against me"[6]— what a support and stronghold is the fact that our God has all power in Heaven and on earth! There is nothing too mighty for Him to manage; there is nothing too insignificant to escape His notice! Jeremiah's faith sees no obstacles, stumbles at no hindrances, faints under no burden, shrinks from no responsibilities because he realizes the sublime Omnipotence of God, and fortifies himself by calling to remembrance His "stretched-out

---

[4] Hard, unbreakable, tough, rocky

[5] Loses strength or weakens

[6] Genesis 42:36: *And Jacob their father said unto them, Me have ye bereaved of my children: Joseph is not, and Simeon is not, and ye will take Benjamin away: all these things are against me.*

arm"[7] in the creation of the Heavens and the earth. Cannot we do likewise?

I took up a book, in a leisure moment, the other day, opened it carelessly, and this is what I read: "It is a scientifically proved fact that this great globe on which we live, spins around on its axis at the rate of a thousand miles an hour, and swings through space in its orbit at a speed immensely greater!"

The words seemed almost to take away my breath! Was I calmly and constantly living in the swirl of such a stupendous miracle as this? Then surely I could say, "Ah, Lord God! there is nothing too hard for Thee. My little troubles and afflictions—how small they must be to You; yet with what tender compassion, do You stoop from guiding the worlds in their courses, to succour[8] and comfort the hearts of those who fear You!"

Never let us give up in despair, while we have such a God to trust in. If there is a great mountain of sorrow or difficulty in your way, dear friend, do not be cast down by the darkness of its shadow. Your God can either make a way for you through it, or He can

---

[7] Psalm 136:12: *With a strong hand, and with a stretched out arm: for his mercy endureth for ever.*
[8] Comfort, help, aid, assistance

guide you around it, or, just as easily, He can carry you right over it! There is nothing too hard for Him! Expect Him to make the crooked things straight, and to bring the high things low;[9] and while you keep humbly at His feet, He will work wondrously, and you shall see His salvation![10]

---

[9] Isaiah 45:2: *I will go before thee, and make the crooked places straight: I will break in pieces the gates of brass, and cut in sunder the bars of iron...*

[10] Luke 3:5-6: *Every valley shall be filled, and every mountain and hill shall be brought low; and the crooked shall be made straight, and the rough ways shall be made smooth; And all flesh shall see the salvation of God.*

Personal Testimony

"My times are in Thy hand!" Psalm 31:15

Why then need I worry or tremble? That great, loving, powerful hand keeps all the events of my life sealed and secure within its almighty clasp! And only He, my Maker and my Master, can permit them to be revealed to me as His will for me. What a compassionate, gracious arrangement! How eminently fitted to fulfill that sweet promise of His Word, "Thou will keep him in perfect peace, whose mind is stayed on Thee, because he trusts in Thee!"[1] If we fully believed this, we would be absolutely devoid of the worry which corrodes[2] and chafes[3] the daily life of so many professing Christians.

"My times." Not one or two important epochs[4] of my history only, but everything that concerns me—joys that I had not expected, sorrows that must have crushed me, if they could have been anticipated, sufferings which

---

[1] Isaiah 26:3: *Thou wilt keep him in perfect peace, whose mind is stayed on thee: because he trusteth in thee.*

[2] Damages, weakens, destroys

[3] Rubs, annoys, irritates

[4] Intervals, ages, periods, times

might have terrified me by their grimness, had I looked upon them, surprises which infinite love had prepared for me, services of which I could not have imagined myself capable—all these lay in that mighty hand as the purposes of God's eternal will for me.

But, as they have developed gradually and silently, how great has been the love which appeared enwrapping and enfolding each one! Has not the grief been measured while the gladness has far more abounded? Have not the comforts and consolations exceeded the crosses and complaints? Have not all things been so arranged, and ordered, and undertaken, and worked out on our behalf that we can but marvel at the goodness and wisdom of God, in meting out from that dear hand of His all the "times" that have passed over us?

You agree with me in all this, do you not, dear reader? Then, I beg you, apply it to your present circumstances, however dark or difficult they may be. They have come direct from your Father's hand to you, and they are His dear will…

So far had I written when, on suddenly, God sent to me a "time" of such severe and prolonged pain, that my pen fell from my fingers, my words and counsels turned their faces inwards, and became a crowd of witnesses—rather than a band of exhorters. I hope they have seen some quiet submission to the will of God, some patience, some restful faith in every detail of God's dealing with me; but, alas! it is easier to know what to do than to do it, and far less courageous to point out the foe's hiding-places than to stand the fire of his artillery. I have been brought very low. The gnawing, tearing teeth of pain have fastened themselves upon me, and night and day I have been held fast in their terrible grip.

"Why does my Lord thus deal with His child?" I asked. I sought to know what lesson He would teach me by this physical suffering which lays me aside from all my beloved work, which feeds me with "the bread of tears," and gives me "tears to drink in great measure."[5]

But no direct answer came to my question, and again and again the lesson was "returned" as yet imperfectly learned. Sometimes, all connected thought vanished, and a bewilderment of sorrow took possession of me; yet not one moment did the great Physician leave me; I was in distress, but never in doubt. Day after day, and night after night, the pain continued; but, often, in my weakness, I

---

[5] Psalm 80:5

remembered what I had been trying to write of before the trial came, and I would whisper, "'My times are in Thy Hand! My times are in Thy hand!' This is Your doing, O Lord, so it must be a right 'time', however sad it may seem to me!"

One day, the post brought a strange, round parcel, which was carried to my bed-side. "Please open it," I said to my friend. This was more easily said than done, the wrappings were so voluminous.[6] At last, a lengthy scroll, beautifully illuminated, was drawn out; and as it was unrolled, it was seen to bear the simple but significant Words—"God Never Makes a Mistake!"

It was as if some sweet far-off echo of God's love had suddenly embodied itself before me. My soul leaped forward to embrace the blessed truth, and found solace and strengthening, as from the hands of a ministering angel. How it soothed and comforted me!

By how small a thing, sometimes, does God send uplifting to His children, when He has cast them down! By how gentle a anodyne[7]

---

[6] Plentiful, abundant
[7] Pain-killer, pain-reliever

can "He give His beloved sleep!"[8] Now, no weakness, or ignorance, or helplessness, or suffering, can prevent me from rejoicing in the fact that "my times" are in the "hand" of a God who never makes a mistake!

---

[8] Psalm 127:2: *It is vain for you to rise up early, to sit up late, to eat the bread of sorrows: for so he giveth his beloved sleep.*

God's Telephone

"My groaning is not hid from Thee." Psalm 38:9

One of the strongest and sweetest consolations which God gives to His sick and afflicted ones, is the assurance that He not only "knows their sorrows,"[1] and tenderly sympathizes with them in their griefs, but that the appointment of every trial proceeds from Him, and that its whole course and continuance are watched by Him with infinite love and care. As a physician keeps his finger on a suffering patient's pulse, that he may know just the limit to which pain may be safely endured, so does our God hold our right hand, while we are passing through the furnaces of trial which lie on our road to Heaven, that He may support us through them, and bring us forth in due time to praise Him for His comforting and sustaining grace!

This text came as a precious cordial to my fainting spirit, as I lately lay upon a bed of

---

[1] Exodus 3:7: And the LORD said, I have surely seen the affliction of my people which are in Egypt, and have heard their cry by reason of their taskmasters; for I know their sorrows...

languishing.[2] Awaking at a very early hour one morning, during my recent illness, I found myself in an extremity of bodily pain and anguish. I tried to pray, but connected[3] thought was an impossibility; groans and tears were the only expression I could give to my suffering; and even these were subdued and hushed, lest the sleeping household should be disturbed.

Then, some blessed, heavenly ministrant[4] whispered the sweet message to my soul, "Your God knows all about you![5] He sees your grief, He hears your groans! There is a telephone from your lips to His heart, and every sigh is recorded there! No darkness, no distance, no dividing distress of any kind can separate you from His constant care. He would spare you every one of these sore pains were it not that He sees that they are working some ultimate blessing for you. Yield yourself absolutely to His will and appointment, and you will find peace even in pain."

So I praised Him with sighs and groans,

---

[2] Wasting away, weakening
[3] Rational
[4] One who serves or waits upon another; a minister
[5] Psalm 139:1-2: *O LORD, thou hast searched me, and known me. Thou knowest my downsitting and mine uprising, thou understandest my thought afar off.*

and in silence; and I felt that the tears which ran down my cheeks were all "put into His bottle,"[6] for He came very near to me, and "as one whom his mother comforts,"[7] so did He comfort me. He did not then remove my pain, but He so strengthened me to endure it, and to rest patiently in Him, that I look back on those hours with joy, as a season of hallowed communion with my God.

To all the Lord's sorrowful and afflicted ones, whether their groans are on account of sin, or sickness, or anguish of heart, I pray that my experience may be an encouragement. Do remember, dear friend, that the God you love, the Master you serve is never indifferent to your grief or unwilling to hear your cry.

> "He knows the meaning of our tears,
> The language of our groans!"[8]

David said truly, "Thou hast considered

---

[6] Psalm 56:8: *Thou tellest my wanderings: put thou my tears into thy bottle: are they not in thy book?*

[7] Isaiah 66:13: *As one whom his mother comforteth, so will I comfort you; and ye shall be comforted in Jerusalem.*

[8] C. H. Spurgeon, *Treasury of David, Vol. II*, (London: Robert Culley, 1871), 222. Psalm 38:9: *Lord, all my desire is before thee; and my groaning is not hid from thee.*

my trouble";[9] and David's God is your God, with the added blessedness of the revelation of Jesus Christ the Savior, whose Divine compassion is as infinite as His power. In time of trouble, the soul is greatly helped by cherishing great thoughts of God; they are sure to induce great longings after Him, great faith in Him, and great love towards Him; and thus, being filled with His fullness, we soar above and beyond all the earthly distractions and disturbances which surround us and seek to cast us down.

Pain, whether bodily, mental, or spiritual, is always unwelcome; and at first sight, wears an aspect which alarms and discomforts us. But it is often an angel in disguise; and many a time we have found that, underneath its terrible exterior, there are hidden the tender smiles of God's love, the gentle discipline of His teaching, and the sweet pity of His marvelous forbearance.

"Give ear to my words, O LORD, consider my meditation." Psalm 5:1

---

[9] Psalm 31:7: *I will be glad and rejoice in thy mercy: for thou hast considered my trouble; thou hast known my soul in adversities...*

The Light of Life!

"Make Thy face to shine upon Thy servant."
Psalm 31:16

As a night without stars, so is my soul, O Lord, if You hide Your face from me! My feet falter, my steps are uncertain, my hands grope as at midnight, my heart is oppressed by an unspeakable fear and dread.

O blessed Light of my life, what has caused You to withdraw Yourself? Why are You hidden behind these thick clouds, so that I cannot rejoice in You?

Alas! my soul, there can be but one answer to your question, and it is a very serious and sorrowful one: "Your iniquities have separated between you and your God, and your sins have made Him hide His face from you!"[1]

O my Lord, this indictment[2] is all too true; but I have acknowledged my transgressions: "I abhor myself, and repent in dust and ashes."[3] I

---

[1] Isaiah 59:2: *But your iniquities have separated between you and your God, and your sins have hid his face from you, that he will not hear.*

[2] Accusation, charge

[3] Job 42:6: *Wherefore I abhor myself, and repent in dust and ashes.*

hate the sin which so constantly surges up within me, defiles my holiest service, and dares intrude even into my prayers.

You know my cry goes daily, almost hourly, up to You: "O Lord, heal me; for my bones are vexed! My soul is also sore vexed: but You, O Lord, how long? Return, O Lord, deliver my soul: oh save me for Your mercies' sake!"[4]

Not for long can such a prayer, if sincere, remain unanswered. The Lord does not love to keep His children in prison. He has but been waiting that the soul's transgression and exceeding need of pardon, should be recognized and confessed, and then He turns to deliver and bless. Mr. Andrew Murray says, "The true victory over sin is this—if the light comes in, the darkness is expelled."[5] Yes, just as the mists and shadows roll away from the sky when the sun is risen upon the earth, so do sins, and griefs, and fears flee before the brightness of the uplifted face of a pardoning

---

[4] Psalm 6:2-4: *Have mercy upon me, O LORD; for I am weak: O LORD, heal me; for my bones are vexed. My soul is also sore vexed: but thou, O LORD, how long? Return, O LORD, deliver my soul: oh save me for thy mercies' sake.*

[5] Andrew Murray (1828-1917), *Absolute Surrender and Other Addresses*, (circa 1897), "Be Filled with the Spirit" (Ephesians 5:18)

God. Lord Jesus, blessed Savior, it is the light of Your reconciled countenance, which I need to "end this grief of sin";[6] it is Your personal presence within my heart, which alone can make my peace flow as a river.[7]

"Make Thy face to shine upon Thy servant."[8] Appear on my behalf, and by Your own almighty power, work the miracle of sun-rising in my soul, scattering the blackness of my sin by the quickening beams of Your matchless love! "My soul waits for the Lord, more than they that watch for the morning."[9]

Waiting soul, is He sure to come? Yes, truly; more surely than that tomorrow's sun will arise upon this world when the hours of darkness have fulfilled their mission, will "the Dayspring from on high"[10] visit those whose

[6] James 4:9: *Be afflicted, and mourn, and weep: let your laughter be turned to mourning, and your joy to heaviness. Humble yourselves in the sight of the Lord, and he shall lift you up.*

[7] Isaiah 48:18: *O that thou hadst hearkened to my commandments! Then had thy peace been as a river, and thy righteousness as the waves of the sea...*

[8] Psalm 119:135: *Make thy face to shine upon thy servant; and teach me thy statutes.*

[9] Psalm 130:5-6: *I wait for the LORD, my soul doth wait, and in his word do I hope. My soul waiteth for the Lord more than they that watch for the morning: I say, more than they that watch for the morning.*

[10] Luke 1:77-79: *To give knowledge of salvation unto his*

eyes are looking, and whose hearts are longing for Him, and His glorious beams of grace.

But there was a time—do you not remember it, O my soul?—when "we hid, as it were, our faces from Him";[11] nay, worse than that, for "He was despised, and we esteemed Him not."[12] What dense blindness was that which saw no beauty in One who is "altogether lovely!"[13]

Rather, far rather, would we be mourning over our distance from Him, and languishing for the manifestation of His sweet presence, than that He should ever again be to us only "as a root out of a dry ground," "without form or loveliness."[14]

Let us thank God for opening our eyes, as

---

people by the remission of their sins, Through the tender mercy of our God; whereby the dayspring from on high hath visited us, To give light to them that sit in darkness and in the shadow of death, to guide our feet into the way of peace.
[11] Isaiah 53:3: *He is despised and rejected of men; a man of sorrows, and acquainted with grief: and we hid as it were our faces from him; he was despised, and we esteemed him not.*
[12] Ibid.
[13] Song of Solomon 5:16: *His mouth is most sweet: yea, he is altogether lovely. This is my beloved, and this is my friend, O daughters of Jerusalem.*
[14] Isaiah 53:2: *For he shall grow up before him as a tender plant, and as a root out of a dry ground: he hath no form nor comeliness; and when we shall see him, there is no beauty that we should desire him.*

a necessary preparation for seeing the light. We would never have prayed, "Lord, make Thy face to shine upon Thy servant,"[15] if we had not seen the "thick cloud"[16] of our transgressions which intervened between Him and our soul's vision of His splendor.

I feel as if I were writing today, for someone whose spiritual experience answers to my own, and I have the hope that such a one will be comforted by "the comfort with which we ourselves are comforted of God."[17] Dear friend, there is no reason why you should remain in the darkness of the Lord's averted[18] face, if you truly long to be restored to His favor. Cry for, and claim, the incoming of the Light of Life. He will be to you "as a light that shines in a dark place";[19] and, before you have

---

[15] Psalm 31:16: *Make thy face to shine upon thy servant: save me for thy mercies' sake.*

[16] Isaiah 44:22: *I have blotted out, as a thick cloud, thy transgressions, and, as a cloud, thy sins: return unto me; for I have redeemed thee.*

[17] II Corinthians 1:3-4: *Blessed be God, even the Father of our Lord Jesus Christ, the Father of mercies, and the God of all comfort; Who comforteth us in all our tribulation, that we may be able to comfort them which are in any trouble, by the comfort wherewith we ourselves are comforted of God.*

[18] Turned away

[19] II Peter 1:19: *We have also a more sure word of prophecy; whereunto ye do well that ye take heed, as unto a light that shineth in a dark place, until the day dawn, and the day star*

finished reading these words, you may hear Him say, "In a little wrath, I hid My face from you for a moment; but with everlasting kindness will I have mercy on you."[20]

"O Light, all light excelling,
Make my heart Your dwelling;
O joy, all grief dispelling—
To this poor heart, come in!"[21]

---

[20] Isaiah 54:8: *In a little wrath I hid my face from thee for a moment; but with everlasting kindness will I have mercy on thee, saith the LORD thy Redeemer.*
[21] Horatius Bonar (1808-1889), hymn "O Light of Light, Shine In"

Grace Asking for More Grace

"Now therefore, I pray Thee, if I have found grace in Thy sight, show me now Thy way, that I may know Thee, that I may find grace in Thy sight."
Exodus 33:13

Moses was in the immediate presence of the Most High when he prayed thus, yet with what holy boldness does he press his suit,[1] and what gracious acceptance does he find at the hands of the Lord! Come, my soul, dare also to use like mighty pleadings. Those were Sinai days, and "law and terrors" were the symbols of God's government; but you are under Calvary's sacred shadow, surely you can ask great things from "the Shepherd of Love"[2] who suffered there for you.

"If I have found grace in Thy sight." If You have loved me from all eternity, and chosen me, a poor sinner, to be Your own pardoned child, I may certainly draw from Your past mercy, a sweet reason for asking You to continue and extend it. My position at this

---

[1] Put forward his case
[2] John 10:14: *I am the good shepherd, and know my sheep, and am known of mine.*

moment, in Your presence, and at Your feet, abundantly proves that I have already found grace in Your sight, or You would not have called me by name, and taught me thus to seek Your favor. And now that I am admitted to the audience-chamber, and You have graciously held out the golden sceptre to me,[3] help me, O Lord, so to present my petition, that You may give me what I ask!

"Show me now Thy way." You know how blind I am by nature, how often I am puzzled and astonished at Your dealings with me, and how frequently the way before me is dark, and hidden, and rough. Throw a ray of heavenly light across all that seems indistinct[4] and gloomy; let "Your way" be illumined by the clear shining of Your love; then how easy and pleasant will it be to walk in it! In days gone by, I have sought and striven to go my own way, and, O Lord, it has been sorry traveling indeed; but now Your grace has made me, not only willing, but determined that my feet shall tread no other path than that which You mark

---

[3] Esther 5:2: *And it was so, when the king saw Esther the queen standing in the court, that she obtained favour in his sight: and the king held out to Esther the golden scepter that was in his hand. So Esther drew near, and touched the top of the scepter.*

[4] Unclear, uncertain, confused

out!

"That I may know Thee." My gracious God, in thus showing me Your way, You must needs draw me closer to You. You will touch my eyes that I may see; You will reveal Yourself to my heart that I may understand Your will; You will permit endearing communings with You which will ravish my soul and be to me a foretaste of Heaven. There have been times when You were as a stranger to me—when Your love was not recognized, nor Your claims regarded; but You have now manifested Yourself, with Divine power, as the Lord and Master of my heart, and I am longing, with intense desire, to know You and the power of Your resurrection!

Lord, there is nothing my heart craves for so passionately as "the light of the knowledge of the glory of God in the face of Jesus Christ."[5] I understand somewhat of Your amazing love and grace—but to be able to plunge into the great deeps of Your covenant mercies—to soar into the limitless space of Your faithfulness—to travel from the East to West of Your pardoning

---

[5] II Corinthians 4:6:*For God, who commanded the light to shine out of darkness, hath shined in our hearts, to give the light of the knowledge of the glory of God in the face of Jesus Christ.*

love,[6] and never find any boundary to Your pity and Your power, this would be to taste of the unspeakable joy[7] which glorified spirits know. Ah! dear Lord, "if I have found grace in Your sight," will You not at least so sweetly reveal Yourself to my waiting heart, that I may be constrained and enabled to exclaim with the spouse in the Canticles, "This is my Beloved, and this is my Friend!"[8]

"That I may find grace in Thy sight." Blessed Master, the more I know of You, the more grace I shall find in Your sight; and when You see anything of Your own likeness in me, You will perfect and complete it. You will draw me, and I shall run after You; and the very fact of following You, will clear my vision, and enlighten my understanding, so that I may see and comprehend more of Your

---

[6] Psalm 103:10-12: *He hath not dealt with us after our sins; nor rewarded us according to our iniquities. For as the heaven is high above the earth, so great is his mercy toward them that fear him. As far as the east is from the west, so far hath he removed our transgressions from us.*

[7] I Peter 1:8: *Whom having not seen, ye love; in whom, though now ye see him not, yet believing, ye rejoice with joy unspeakable and full of glory: Receiving the end of your faith, even the salvation of your souls.*

[8] Song of Solomon 5:16: *His mouth is most sweet: yea, he is altogether lovely. This is my beloved, and this is my friend, O daughters of Jerusalem.*

beauty and preciousness—more of Your marvelous grace to me. You know that everything of earth tends to hide my Lord from me; Satan envelopes me in dark clouds of unbelief; my own sinful heart blinds me; cares oppress and crush me; and carnal fears gather round, intent on my bewilderment. But, loving Savior, "if I have found grace in Thy sight," nothing can separate me from You; You have taken my hand in Yours, and through all dangers, over all difficulties, and in spite of all enemies, You will lead and guide me safely home to Yourself. Therefore, "I pray, if I have found grace in Thy sight—show me now Thy way—that I may know Thee—that I may find grace in Thy sight."

All Grace Abounding

"God is able to make all grace abound toward you,
that ye, always having all sufficiency in all things,
may abound to every good work."
2 Corinthians 9:8

What a treasure-trove is here for poverty-stricken souls! If our faith were but strong and eager enough to gather up the riches stored in this chest of blessing—what millionaires in grace we might become!

"But the chest is fast locked," you say, "how can we grasp what we cannot see?" True, yet faith is the key which not only unlocks these treasures, but gives us the right to claim them as our own, and use them to the constant enrichment of our daily life.

I do not know how it is with you, my dear readers, but when I look upon such an exhibition of Divine possibilities as is contained in this and similar portions of God's Word, I wonder, with a sore amazement, at my own spiritual condition, which, far too often, is reduced to one of indigence[1] and distress. The grand assurance, here given by the apostle, of

---

[1] Great poverty; lack of food, clothing, necessities of life

our God's ability to supply all our need,[2] is no new thing to us. We know that He "is able to make all grace abound toward us,"[3] we fully recognize the blessedness of "always having all sufficiency in all things,"[4] we desire intensely to "abound to every good work,"[5] but few of us have joyfully entered upon this inheritance. We have not yet taken possession of the land; we may have cut a cluster or two of its fruit,[6] and eaten a mouthful or so of its honey;[7] but our faith has not yet dared to claim the fulfillment of that wonderful promise, "Every place that the sole of your foot shall tread upon, that have I given unto you."[8]

O come, all you longing souls, come, poor

---

[2] Philippians 4:19:*But my God shall supply all your need according to his riches in glory by Christ Jesus.*

[3] II Corinthians 9:8: *And God is able to make all grace abound toward you, that ye, always having all sufficiency in all things, may abound to every good work...*

[4] Ibid.

[5] Ibid.

[6] Numbers 13:23: *And they came unto the brook of Eshcol, and cut down from thence a branch with one cluster of grapes, and they bare it between two upon a staff; and they brought of the pomegranates, and of the figs.*

[7] Numbers 13:27: *And they told him, and said, We came unto the land whither thou sentest us, and surely it floweth with milk and honey; and this is the fruit of it.*

[8] Joshua 1:3: *Every place that the sole of your foot shall tread upon, that have I given unto you, as I said unto Moses.*

doubting reader, come, weak and trembling writer, gird up the loins of your mind,[9] and let your faith march boldly into this promised land, never again to leave it until it is exchanged for the heavenly Canaan!

Think for a moment how wealthy we should be, could we but thus believe in our God. What could we not be, and do, and suffer, if all grace abounded toward us? With what persistency and impressiveness, does the apostle repeat the word "all"—that little word with so vast a meaning! Can we imagine the bliss of possessing all grace—always (or all ways), and having all sufficiency—in all things?

I lay down my pen for a moment to thank God for these riches of grace in Christ Jesus my Lord, and I take it up again with this thought in my heart—

"What more can He say, than to you He has said,
You, who unto Jesus for refuge have fled?"[10]

---

[9] I Peter 1:13: *Wherefore gird up the loins of your mind, be sober, and hope to the end for the grace that is to be brought unto you at the revelation of Jesus Christ...*
[10] John Rippon (1751-1836), English Baptist minister and hymn writer, "How Firm a Foundation"

There is another sense in which the words of this text may come home to us. The apostle Paul, in previous verses, had been stirring up the Christians in Corinth to liberality of spirit, and zeal in ministering to the saints. It is noteworthy that he brings abounding grace and generous giving into very close connection, linking them together as cause and effect, even as the plentiful sowing of the seed ensures a bounteous harvest. He says, in effect, "Your God is so immensely rich, and so anxious to enrich you, not with grace alone, but with gifts of all things' that the more you give, the more you will have. And if you purpose in your heart to be bountiful, giving love, money, help, and kindness, to all around you—God, who loves a cheerful giver,[11] will see to it that you have the means of carrying out your desire, for you shall have 'all sufficiency of "all things" that you "may abound to every good work."[12]

---

[11] II Corinthians 9:6-7: *But this I say, He which soweth sparingly shall reap also sparingly; and he which soweth bountifully shall reap also bountifully. Every man according as he purposeth in his heart, so let him give; not grudgingly, or of necessity: for God loveth a cheerful giver.*

[12] II Corinthians 9:8: *And God is able to make all grace abound toward you; that ye, always having all sufficiency in all things, may abound to every good work...*

I think this is a very grave and important view of the text, for may it not be that we, who complain of being "straitened"[13] for this very reason, that we have lacked zeal in enriching others? Perhaps we have forgotten that "the worldling prospers by laying up, the Christian by laying out."[14] Beloved, if in this "our heart condemns us, God is greater than our heart, and knows all things."[15] Let us seek earnestly from Him the power to "abound in this grace also."[16]

"God is able,"[17] dear friends, and He is as willing as He is able, "to make all grace abound

---

[13] Distressed, needy

[14] Luke 12:19-21: *And I will say to my soul, Soul, thou hast much goods laid up for many years; take thine ease, eat, drink, and be merry. But God said unto him, Thou fool, this night thy soul shall be required of thee: then whose shall those things be, which thou hast provided? So is he that layeth up treasure for himself, and is not rich toward God.*

[15] I John 3:18-20: *My little children, let us not love in word, neither in tongue; but in deed and in truth. And hereby we know that we are of the truth, and shall assure our hearts before him. For if our heart condemn us, God is greater than our heart, and knoweth all things.*

[16] II Corinthians 8:7: *Therefore, as ye abound in every thing, in faith, and utterance, and knowledge, and in all diligence, and in your love to us, see that ye abound in this grace also.*

[17] Ephesians 3:20: *Now unto him that is able to do exceeding abundantly above all that we ask or think, according to the power that worketh in us...*

toward you."[18] There is no need for any child of His to be destitute, or distressed, either in spiritual or temporal matters. Does this assertion startle you? Yet God's Word bears it out; and the fact that there are so many half-starved Christians, poor in faith, penniless in comfort, leading unlovely and joyless lives, does not alter it in the least.

"He is able!" Say it over and over to yourself till you learn its blessed music; it will encourage your souls against every sort of despair. You are very sinful—yes, but, "He is able to save to the uttermost."[19] You are weakest of the weak—true, but, "He is able to keep you from falling."[20] You are subject to fierce temptations—but, "He is able to succour them that are tempted."[21] You tremble lest you should not endure to the end—ah! but, "He is

---

[18] II Corinthians 9:8: *And God is able to make all grace abound toward you; that ye, always having all sufficiency in all things, may abound to every good work...*

[19] Hebrews 7:25: *Wherefore he is able also to save them to the uttermost that come unto God by him, seeing he ever liveth to make intercession for them.*

[20] Jude 24-25: *Now unto him that is able to keep you from falling, and to present you faultless before the presence of his glory with exceeding joy, To the only wise God our Saviour, be glory and majesty, dominion and power, both now and ever. Amen.*

[21] Hebrews 2:18: *For in that he himself hath suffered being tempted, he is able to succour them that are tempted.*

able to present you faultless before the presence of His glory, with exceeding joy."[22] Is not this enough?

Listen, dear soul, the Master Himself says to you, "Believe ye that I am able to do this?"[23] See to it that your heart answers, "Yes, Lord," and then His sweet response will be, "According to your faith, be it unto you."[24]

---

[22] Jude 24-25—see above
[23] Matthew 9:28: *And when he was come into the house the blind men came to him: and Jesus saith unto them, Believe ye that I am able to do this? They said unto him, Yea, Lord.*
[24] Matthew 9:29: *Then touched he their eyes, saying, According to your faith be it unto you.*

A Honeycomb of Delight

"Because the LORD loved you!"
Deuteronomy 7:8

My gracious God, there is a honeycomb of delight and sweetness in these words. Will You put the rod of faith into my hand, this morning, and enable me to dip the end thereof into this rich provision, that my soul may eat, and be satisfied,[1] and that the eyes of my understanding may be enlightened?[2]

"Because the Lord loved you!" This is His great "reason" for all His dealings with His own people. It is a full and convincing answer to all the doubts and questionings with which Satan can perplex and distress the Lord's timid ones. The enemy of souls has, alas! a powerful confederate in the wicked unbelief which lurks within us; but they will both be vanquished

---

[1] I Samuel 14:27: *But Jonathan heard not when his father charged the people with the oath: wherefore he put forth the end of the rod that was in his hand, and dipped it in an honeycomb, and put his hand to his mouth; and his eyes were enlightened.*

[2] Ephesians 1:18: *The eyes of your understanding being enlightened; that ye may know what is the hope of his calling, and what the riches of the glory of his inheritance in the saints...*

when we have learned to use this weapon of war against them.

Come, my heart, try its blessed force and quality at this moment! The foe says, "Why does God send you affliction, and sorrow, and suffering, when those who do not fear His Name have continual quietness and abounding prosperity?"[3]

If you can boldly answer, "It is because the Lord loves me," then you will have given him such a sword-thrust as will free you, for a time, at least, from his cunning devices and fierce onslaughts.

Or, look at the text as a shaft of sunlight, piercing through a chink in the shuttered window of some dark experience. Bring your fears and forebodings out of the dusky corners, and place them within the radiance of this light of love. You will be amazed to see them transformed into confident trusts: your doubts will vanish as if they had never been, and the evil and bitter things of life will all be transformed into blessings in a moment.

"Because the Lord loved you" is the

---

[3] Psalm 73:2-3: *But as for me, my feet were almost gone; my steps had well nigh slipped. For I was envious at the foolish, when I saw the prosperity of the wicked.*

master-key which fits the wards[4] of the hardest question, and opens the mysteries of the deepest problem! It is a talisman[5] of wondrous efficacy,[6] and every believer in the Lord Jesus Christ may not only rejoice in its possession, but use it constantly to obtain all the desire of his heart in spiritual things.

"What aileth thee,"[7] poor soul? Is it loss of health, or friends, or means? Has God taken from you some dearly-loved one, and left you alone on this sad earth? Is He trying and proving you, by many and varied tests and troubles, "to know what was in your heart"?[8] Whatever may be your immediate and peculiar sorrow, if you have grace and faith enough to say, "This is because the Lord loves me," I dare to promise you that all the bitterness of the affliction will melt away, and the peace of God

---

[4] Rooms, areas

[5] Charm

[6] Effectiveness; ability to bring about a desired effect

[7] Genesis 21:17: *And God heard the voice of the lad; and the angel of God called to Hagar out of heaven, and said unto her, What aileth thee, Hagar? Fear not; for God hath heard the voice of the lad where he is.*

[8] Deuteronomy 8:2: *And thou shalt remember all the way which the LORD thy God led thee these forty years in the wilderness, to humble thee, and to prove thee, to know what was in thine heart, whether thou wouldest keep his commandments, or no.*

will fill you with a sweet content which passes understanding.[9] No distress can withstand such Divine solace, no anguish can refuse the relief of this balm of Gilead.[10] If all that happens to you can be traced directly or indirectly to the hand of your loving Lord, then how gladly should you bear life's burdens, and how perfect should be the rest in which heart and mind should dwell!

O gracious Master, looking back over the years that are gone, the interminglings of grief and gladness pass before my eyes as the clouds sail by on an April day; and though the memories of great affliction and sore bereavement cast deep shadows across the scene, and seem for a time to blot out all the brightness, yet, above and beyond those changeful skies, the sun has never ceased shining, and darkness as well as day has proclaimed the immutability of Your love. When the ears of my soul are attuned to catch the soft whisper of Your voice, I hear You saying: "All this, My child, was because the

---

[9] Philippians 4:7: *And the peace of God, which passeth all understanding, shall keep your hearts and minds through Christ Jesus.*

[10] Heals, soothes; Jeremiah 8:22: *Is there no balm in Gilead; is there no physician there? Why then is not the health of the daughter of my people recovered?*

Lord loved you! Left to yourself; you would have destroyed yourself; but in Me was your help found. All the tribulations you have endured were but My servants to whom I entrusted the necessary discipline of your earthly life. "

Do not forget those words of Mine: "As many as I love, I rebuke and chasten!"[11]

---

[11] Revelation 3:19: *As many as I love, I rebuke and chasten: be zealous therefore, and repent.*

A Blessed Paradox

"I have seen his ways, and will heal him!"
Isaiah 57:18

Here is one of the blessedly incomprehensible paradoxes[1] of God's love and mercy, which startles us by its excess of compassionate grace: "I have seen his ways, and"—one would have thought the next sentence must be, "I will punish him," or at least, "I will rebuke him." But, instead of wrath, here is pardon; pity makes room for love; and in the place of bitterness, the Lord gives a blessing! "I have seen his ways, and will heal him!"

O wanderer, will not these tender words cause you to return to your Lord? O stony heart, will you not break at so loving a touch as this? O cold and half-dead soul, will not such a Divine cordial[2] revive you?

"I have seen his ways." What "ways" has God seen in you? Have they not been "wicked,"

---

[1] Contradiction, mystery, puzzle, riddle

[2] Cordial: a sweetened drink or a medicine that gives energy and feeling of well-being/Elixir: a sweet substance, usually in liquid form that is used in medicines; can refer to "magical potions"; a remedy

"crooked," "perverse,"[3] "your own ways"—"the ways of death?" Have you not turned aside from the path of life, and refused to walk "in all His way,"[4] and chosen "a stubborn way"[5] for yourself?

Our heart must give a sad assent to all these charges. As we bow humbly before Him, and say, "You are acquainted with all my ways,"[6] we feel that such knowledge of us on His part, intensifies our wonder and gratitude at the loving compassion with which He regards us.

When I was a little child, and had been troublesome to my mother, reproof or punishment would always be followed by the trembling question, "Mother, don't you love me?" And my mother's reply invariably was, "Yes, I do love you; but I do not love your naughty ways!" Poor mother! Doubtless I tried her very much, and this was the best that grieved parental love could say. But the

---

[3] Improper, wicked, immoral, obstinate, hard-headed

[4] Psalm 128:1-2: *Blessed is every one that feareth the LORD; that walketh in his way. For thou shall eat the labour of thine hands: happy shalt thou be, and it shall be well with thee.*

[5] Isaiah 66:3b: *Yea, they have chosen their own ways, and their soul delighteth in their abominations.*

[6] Psalm 139:3: *Thou compassest my path and my lying down, and art acquainted with all my ways.*

Heavenly Father has sweeter, choicer words than these for His erring children.

His love is Divine; so He says, "I have seen his ways, and will heal him." O sweet pitifulness of our God! O tenderness inexplicable! O love surpassing all earth's loveliest affection! Do not our hard hearts yield under the power of such compassion as this?

God knows all our wickedness; He has seen all our waywardness; yet His purpose towards us is one of healing and pardon and not of anger and putting away.

As I learn more of God, I get so sick of sin—indwelling-sin, heart-sin, I mean—both in myself and others—that my soul welcomes this Word of the Lord, as a condemned prisoner embraces a reprieve,[7] or as a drowning man clutches the life-buoy thrown out for his rescue. To be healed of the disease which wastes us, to be delivered from the deadness and indifference which enchain us, to have a perfect heart with the Lord our God, and to walk before Him in a perfect way, this, I take it, is the blessed prospect held out by this promise. Who will claim its fulfillment at once? Who will take our gracious God at His Word, and believingly receive the priceless blessing

---

[7] Pardon

which His love offers?

O blessed Lord, Your forbearance[8] with us in the past has been a miracle of mercy! You have seen so much in us which Your soul has abhorred, and yet You come now with this gift of healing in Your hands, which means not only pardon, but the power to be holy.

Lord, we lift up empty, beseeching hands to Your full ones; lay upon them, we pray, all that they can bear of Your promised blessing! Our own ways have led us farther and farther from You; now let Your forgiving, healing love draw us so close to You, that we can never again be among those "who leave the paths of uprightness, to walk in the ways of darkness."[9]

---

[8] Patience, sympathy, mercy

[9] Proverbs 2:10-13: *When wisdom entereth into thine heart, and knowledge is pleasant unto thy soul; Discretion shall preserve thee, understanding shall keep thee: To deliver thee from the way of the evil man, from the man that speaketh froward things; Who leave the paths of uprightness, to walk in the ways of darkness...*

Divine Strengthening

"I will strengthen thee; yea, I will help thee"
Isaiah 41:10

Who will come with me to the King this morning, to lay at His feet a petition for the fulfillment of this Word of His grace, upon which He has caused us to hope? We shall be a company of Feeble-minds, and Much-afraids, and Fearings, and Ready-to-halts;[1] and we may make but a sorry appearance in His courts. But our necessities admit of no delay, and this King is so gracious, and has so much love and pity for weak and needy ones that He is sure to grant us, not an audience merely, but according to the desire of our heart. My own condition is such that I must have His help, or faint, and utterly fail; and I know there are many in like stress of need who will seek the King's face with me.

Blessed be His Name, we may come into His presence with holy boldness[2] and

---

[1] John Bunyan, *The Pilgrim's Progress, Part II*—these are characters who joined with Christiana, her family, and Mr. Great-heart in their journey to the Celestial City
[2] Hebrews 4:16: *Let us therefore come boldly unto the throne of grace, that we may obtain mercy, and find grace to help in*

confidence, bringing with us the warrant of our faith in His own precious promise, fairly and legibly written on the pages of His Word, without blot or erasure, and with no "ifs "and "buts "to mar its sublime simplicity: "I will strengthen you; yea, I will help you." Does He not love to be trusted? Does He not honor faith? Can one word of His good promise ever fail, or shall not the thing which He has said, surely come to pass?[3]

And, as to our present need of succor,[4] some of us can say, with tear-filled eyes, "O Lord, if weakness be a plea for Your promised strength, then are we truly fit objects of Your mercy; for we are at the lowest ebb of helplessness; we have scarcely strength enough left to feel that we are feeble; we are 'brought into the dust of death.'"[5] God has "weakened our strength in the way,"[6] to teach us our dependence upon Himself. He has humbled

---

time of need.

[3] Isaiah 14:24: *The LORD of hosts hath sworn, saying, Surely as I have thought, so shall it come to pass; and as I have purposed, so shall it stand...*

[4] Assistance, aid, support

[5] Psalm22:15: *My strength is dried up like a potsherd; and my tongue cleaveth to my jaws; and thou hast brought me into the dust of death.*

[6] Psalm 102:23: *He weakened my strength in the way; he shortened my days.*

us, that He may lift us up. He has shown us our own nothingness, that He may be our All-in-all.

Most of us have needed this discipline of complete failure in ourselves to convince us that our strength is in God alone! He has had to humble us, and to prove us, to know what is in our heart; and, alas! with some of us, it has taken as long a time to do this as in the days of old, when the Lord's people wandered in the wilderness for forty years before they learned the lesson. Ah! what trouble our God takes with us! What ungrateful, perverse,[7] rebellious children we have been! He has had to empty us of so much that is abominable in His sight— our pride, our self-sufficiency, our carnal security,[8] our own righteousness—before He could fill us with His Spirit, and take pleasure in us, that it is no wonder the process has been a painful one, and cost us many a cry and groan. We have been cast headlong from the heights of our pride and self-exaltation; and then, as we lay bruised and bleeding on the ground of self-abasement, crushed under a sense of our own utter weakness, the Lord has

---

[7] Unreasonable, uncooperative, stubborn
[8] Security in the human senses, security in worldly or human power

drawn near, and given this gracious assurance, "I will strengthen thee; yea, I will help thee." *For I the LORD thy God will hold thy right hand, saying unto thee, Fear not; I will help thee* (Isaiah 41:13).

But how shall I describe the joy with which we caught the first soft whisper of His tender voice, and recognized the strength-giving touch of His mighty hand? "I was brought low," we said—the words were scarcely audible; we were so weak—but faith touched our lips with a cordial, and then, loud and clear from our unloosened tongue, rang out the triumphant testimony, "and He helped me!"[9]

Is it not wonderful, the incoming of Divine strength into an empty heart? Now we know by experience what the apostle meant when he wrote, "He said unto me: My grace is sufficient for you; for My strength is made perfect in weakness."[10] Here we have the same Promiser and the same promise—but in other words. "I will strengthen thee." "I, the Almighty God, whose power is infinite, will strengthen you, a

---

[9] Psalm 116:6: *The LORD preserveth the simple: I was brought low, and he helped me.*

[10] II Corinthians 12:9: *And he said unto me, My grace is sufficient for thee: for my strength is made perfect in weakness. Most gladly therefore will I rather glory in my infirmities, that the power of Christ may rest upon me.*

poor worm of the dust!"

Oh, the condescension and tenderness of our God! Our extremity is His opportunity; His mercy follows hard after our misery; and as soon as He has taught us our exceeding need, He supplies it with the bounties of His exceeding love. Then it is, that He gives us "beauty for ashes, the oil of joy for mourning, and the garment of praise for the spirit of heaviness!"[11] And, oh! with what joyful hearts and shining eyes do we afterwards walk in the light of His countenance! "Dear Lord," we say, "it is worth while being weak, to be thus gloriously strengthened by You!"

---

[11] Isaiah 61:3: *To appoint unto them that mourn in Zion, to give unto them beauty for ashes, the oil of joy for mourning, the garment of praise for the spirit of heaviness; that they might be called trees of righteousness, the planting of the LORD, that he might be glorified.*

The Touch of Faith

"Who touched Me?...Somebody hath touched Me." Luke 8:45, 46

"Master, the multitudes throng You and press against You; and yet You say: Who touched Me?"[1] In all that vast surging crowd of people, jostling each other in order to get a view of the wonderful Man in their midst, and even pressing upon Him in their rude inquisitiveness, there was but one poor suffering woman who understood His mission, and tested for herself the power she believed Him to possess.

Blessed Lord Jesus, this sick and sorrowful "somebody" shall be my guide to Your feet, this morning! I rejoice to know that her touch of faith must have been the result of Your own Divine love and compassion. Your hand must have moved her heart, or her finger would never have been laid on the hem of Your garment. You must have awakened within her,

---

[1] Luke 8:45-46: *And Jesus said, Who touched me? When all denied, Peter and they that were with him said, Master, the multitude throng thee and press thee, and sayest thou, Who touched me? And Jesus said, Somebody hath touched me: for I perceive that virtue is gone out of me.*

the desire and the trust which produced such happy results. This "somebody's" sad case, dear Lord, was well known to You, and, "for the sake of them that stood by,"[2] as well as a sweet incentive to all those who should hereafter believe on Your Name, You did graciously draw this sin-sick, soul-sick, unclean creature to You, that You might bestow on her both pardon and healing![3]

Oh! will You not repeat the miracle at this moment, Lord? Both writer and reader are needing the exercise of Your Omnipotent power on their behalf, and are now stretching forth trembling hands of faith to receive the blessing which You alone can give! O bid us touch and live!

Do you wonder, poor sinner, whether your need, and your longings, and your first faint

---

[2] John 11:41-42: *Then they took away the stone from the place where the dead was laid. And Jesus lifted up his eyes, and said, Father, I thank thee that thou hast heard me. And I knew that thou hearest me always: but because of the people which stand by I said it, that they may believe that thou hast sent me.*

[3] Luke 8:47-48: *And when the woman saw that she was not hid, she came trembling, and falling down before him, she declared unto him before all the people for what cause she had touched him, and how she was healed immediately. And he said unto her, Daughter, be of good comfort: thy faith hath made thee whole; go in peace.*

hopes of mercy are known to the dear Savior whom you seek? See here how instantly the Lord was aware of a touch upon the edge of His robe, and how immediately He knew that virtue (power) was gone out of Him. What strong encouragement this should give to a timid, shrinking soul!

The slightest contact of faith with Christ, ensures salvation. So full is He of blessed power and willingness to save, that, even from His raiment,[4] the sacred healing flowed, in response to this poor woman's trustful touch. How much more will spiritual cleanliness be bestowed on you when you say—

> "My faith doth lay her hand
> On that dear head of Thine,
> While like a penitent I stand,
> And here confess my sin."[5]

I want to cheer my own soul with this comfort of God. I am realizing very painfully that "in me dwelleth no good thing";[6] nay,

---

[4] Clothing, robe

[5] Isaac Watts (1674-1748), hymn writer called the "Father of English Hymnody"; *My faith would lay her hand On that dear head of Thine, While like a penitent I stand, And there confess my sin.*

[6] Romans 7:18: *For I know that in me (that is, in my flesh,)*

more, that "evil is present with me."[7] The fight against inbred corruption is fierce, and I am well-near spent in the struggle. Is not this the very time to test and trust the Savior's power? I shall have to force my way through a crowd of iniquities, and doubts, and discouragements; but mine is an urgent case, and I know that, "if I may touch but His clothes, I shall be whole."[8] For so surely as my faith meets my Savior's free grace, my deliverance is assured and complete. Ah! how insensate[9] and ignorant it would be to draw back in full view of life eternal, and choose to perish rather than to persist!

"But," says one, "I think I could more easily push my way through a crowd of people, and really reach out my hand to touch Jesus, than I can spiritually and mentally imitate that woman's action." Yes, I see, you are an unbelieving Thomas;[10] you must put your

---

dwelleth no good thing: for to will is present with me; but how to perform that which is good I find not.

[7] Romans 7:21: *I find then a law, that, when I would do good, evil is present with me.*

[8] Mark 5:27-28: *When she had heard of Jesus, came in the press behind, and touched his garment. For she said, If I may touch but his clothes, I shall be whole.*

[9] Lacking understanding, unfeeling, foolish

[10] John 20:24-25:*But Thomas, one of the twelve, called Didymus, was not with them when Jesus came. The other*

finger in the print of the nails, and thrust your hand into His side, ere you believe. This always has seemed to me a willful and hard-hearted resolve on the part of the apostle, yet how tenderly the Lord dealt with it, how fully and freely He gave Thomas leave[11] to set his doubts at rest in his own way![12] I do not think he availed himself of the permission; the glory of the Savior's risen body scattered all his skepticism in a moment; but there was gentle reproof in Christ's after-word, "Because you have seen Me, you have believed—blessed are those who have not seen, and yet have believed."[13]

O my gracious Lord, it is a marvel of marvels that You did allow my faith to draw forth Your Divine power to heal and save! It is sweet comfort to remember that You knew all about that silent woman, stealthily creeping up

---

disciples therefore said unto him, We have seen the Lord. But he said unto them, Except I shall see in his hands the print of the nails, and put my finger into the print of the nails, and thrust my hand into his side, I will not believe.

[11] Permission

[12] John 20:27: *Then saith he to Thomas, Reach hither thy finger, and behold my hands; and reach hither thy hand, and thrust it into my side: and be not faithless, but believing.*

[13] John 20:29: *Jesus saith unto him, Thomas, because thou hast seen me, thou hast believed: blessed are they that have not seen, and yet have believed.*

behind You, to snatch a blessing even from Your garment; but it is still greater solace to understand that You did permit her feeble finger to unlock, as it were, the sluices[14] of Your eternal love, so that spirit, soul, and body were at once flooded with heavenly grace and favor, and with perfect peace and pardon! O Lord Jesus, words fail me to extol Your wondrous compassion, Your unspeakable pity and love; but do, I beseech You, now draw some other poor sad "somebodies" to Your dear feet, that they, too, may be made whole!

---

[14] Floodgate, a gate that holds back water

Toiling in Rowing
(A New Year's Message)

"He saw them toiling in rowing" Mark 6:48

Beloved friends,

It may be that, for some of you, the New Year opens in sadness and silence, without the merry crash of bells, and the welcoming cheers which celebrate its advent, and signify its joy to so many other hearts. Your trials are heavy; your comforts are few; earthly sorrows weigh you down and hinder the glad mounting of your spirit to heavenly places in Christ Jesus. The prospect of incessant toil and weariness oppresses you, or the retrospect[1] of sorrow and suffering has benumbed[2] you, and you do not feel you can heartily respond to the usual salutation of friend to friend, "I wish you a Happy New Year!" You would rather have done with earth, and that God gave you the wings of a dove, that you might fly away and be at rest.[3]

---

[1] Looking back to the past, reviewing the past
[2] To make numb, unable to feel
[3] Psalm 55:6: *And I said, Oh that I had wings like a dove! for then would I fly away, and be at rest.*

I quite understand your feelings; I have fellowship with you in your fear and faintness of heart; but I bring afresh to you today, the sweet and comforting assurance that your blessed Lord knows all your sorrows, sees all your sufferings, is watching over you with a Divine love and care which know no cessation,[4] and will, in His own good time, either relieve or release you.

Nay, do you not know that, sometimes, the Master brings His dear ones into sore straits, with the express object of manifesting His mighty power in their deliverance? Let me try to show you this, as in a picture, roughly outlined from the pages of God's Word.

Do you see that small ship on a wind-swept lake? Storm and darkness are fast gathering their forces together, the sea is tossing and raging in passionate response to the war-cry of the tempest, and serious danger is menacing the men in the frail vessel. They are straining every nerve and muscle to make for the opposite shore, they labor at the oars with almost superhuman strength; but they are no match against the tremendous force of wind and wave which beats them back continually, and threatens to engulf them. Your heart fails

---

[4] Ending, finishing, stopping

you as you look on their perilous position, and you expect every moment that the sea will swallow up its prey.

But now turn your gaze landwards. On the brow of an adjacent hill stands a solitary, but majestic Man. He is intently watching the rowers in that trembling, storm-tossed bark.[5] Not a danger is overlooked, not an effort is unnoticed, not a fear in their hearts that does not thrill His soul with pity, and appeal to His tenderest love. He is going to save them; and in the manner of their deliverance, He will gloriously manifest His own Divine power and goodness. He will presently tread under His feet the waves of that turbulent sea, and compel those fierce gales to quail before Him in silent homage. [6]

You know the sweet and sacred story; but I want you to realize that it is your story, too, and that, just as truly as "He saw them toiling in rowing," and knew every detail of their condition and jeopardy, so does He take note of your sorrows, your difficulties, your need of His help and presence.

Though you are tossed about on the rough waves of adverse circumstances, and every

---

[5] Boat, ship
[6] Matthew 14:22-33; Mark 6:45-52; John 6: 15-21

wind that blows seems contrary, though all
your efforts do not bring you to the desired
haven, and your strength seems fast failing—
do not lose courage; remember that your Lord
is very near, and that, at the right hour and
moment, He will come to your relief, and
deliver you out of all your distresses.

If those disciples had known that their
blessed Master was watching them, and caring
for them, and coming to them, do you not
think they would have shipped their oars,[7]
defied the tempest to do its worst, and sung
songs of deliverance amidst the surges of the
storm? They did not know or understand, for
the Word says, "their hearts were hardened,"[8]
and so they toiled on even to exhaustion, and
failed to recognize the Lord even when they
saw Him.

But, dear friends, "Ye know the grace of
our Lord Jesus Christ";[9] and therefore it should
be easy for you to trust Him, no matter how
roughly the wind blows, or how fiercely the
storm drives. Take this blessed comfort right

---

[7] To place the oars in the rowlocks
[8] Mark 6:52: *For they considered not the miracle of the loaves: for their heart was hardened.*
[9] II Corinthians 8:9: *For ye know the grace of our Lord Jesus Christ, that, though he was rich, yet for your sakes he became poor, that ye through his poverty might be rich.*

into your heart, that your Lord so truly cares for you that nothing which concerns you is unimportant to Him, or unnoticed by Him. Live as in His immediate presence. Accustom yourself to watch for the guidance of His eye, and the ready help of His hand. Believe with all your soul and strength in His everlasting love; and then, give up "toiling in rowing," and sit in your boat and sing—

"Peace from every trial flows,
Because I know that Jesus knows."[10]

---

[10] Frances Ridley Havergal (1836-1879), English hymn writer and poet: *I know the sorrow that is known To the tear-burdened heart alone; But now I know its full relief Through Him who was acquaint with grief, And peace through every trial flows, Because I know that Jesus knows.*

In Darkness, Without Jesus

"It was now dark, and Jesus was not come to them." John 6:17

As this text is read, I think I can hear some sorrowful soul say, "That exactly expresses my condition. I am sorely troubled and depressed; I see no light; and the dear Lord, who used to be so near, has withdrawn Himself from me." Shall we talk the matter over, dear reader, and try to find out why you are in the dark, and why Jesus does not come?

The first question is, "How came you there?" Did the darkness fall upon you from natural causes, as the night overtook these disciples in the boat? Or, did the Lord bid you enter into the cloud? Is your gloom brought about by the deep shadows of bodily infirmity? Or, have you willfully closed your eyes, and thus shut out the light of Heaven? Give us now Your wondrous "Search-light," O Spirit of God, that we may see our own true position!

"It was now dark." The shadows of evening were already falling when the disciples left the shore, so the night naturally came upon them before they reached "the other side."[1] We do not read that they were afraid of the darkness; but they had left their Master on the mountain-top, they were lonely and perplexed in His absence, and perhaps they were wondering when and where they should next see Him.

Something like this may be your present experience. It is night in your soul because Jesus is away; your heart mourns for Him, and refuses to be comforted till once again the light of His face is lifted up upon you. Be of good cheer, dear friend, if you are thus longing for Him, the darkness will soon be past, and the Dayspring[2] will arise in your heart. He is already on the way to you, walking on the waves of your unrest and sorrow; and it shall be all well with you when He reveals Himself by that sweet word, "It is I, be not afraid!"[3]

"It was now dark." Sometimes, God sends His children into the dark. The dispensations of darkness, which try the Lord's people, are

---

[1] John 6:15-22

[2] Dawn, daybreak, sunrising; Luke 1:77-79: *To give knowledge of salvation unto his people by the remission of their sins, Through the tender mercy of our God; whereby the dayspring from on high hath visited us, To give light to them that sit in darkness and in the shadow of death, to guide our feet into the way of peace.*

[3] John 6:20: *But he saith unto them, It is I; be not afraid.*

often His appointment and purpose. An old writer says: "The uses of darkness are manifold: to humble us; to convince us of our absolute helplessness; to prove to us our momentary[4] need of Divine sustaining; to make Christ alone the ground of our hope, and the object of our boasting, by bringing the soul off from everything else, that it may look only to Him."[5]

What must you do if God is thus dealing with you? You must "trust, and not be afraid."[6] "Rest in the Lord, and wait patiently for Him."[7] His hand will lead you through the darkness into the light, and all the more quickly if you constantly tell Him how sorely your heart aches with the longing to see again the sunshine of His love. Be assured that He will not leave you comfortless, He will come to you.[8]

_____

[4] Moment by moment

[5] D. A. Doudney, Curate of Bonmahon, *The Gospel Magazine; and Protestant Beacon*, (Ireland: Bonmahon Industrial Printing School, 1853), January, 1853, 47.

[6] Isaiah 12:2: *Behold, God is my salvation; I will trust, and not be afraid: for the LORD JEHOVAH is my strength and my song; he also is become my salvation.*

[7] Psalm 37:7: *Rest in the LORD, and wait patiently for him: fret not thyself because of him who prospereth in his way, because of the man who bringeth wicked devices to pass.*

[8] John 14:18: *I will not leave you comfortless: I will come to*

"It was now dark." There is a darkness which may easily be traced to bodily ailments, and a disordered frame. Depression of spirit is frequently the outcome of oppression of the flesh. Physical weakness is sometimes the cause of decrease of spiritual power. And then it is that Satan, ever on the alert to vex, if he cannot harm us, takes advantage of our sad condition to insinuate doubts and fears which we should not tolerate when in vigorous health. He is at home in the darkness, and he peoples it with fancies and phantoms which intensify its blackness. Our souls are like frightened children in a dark room, we tremble and are afraid; but we can cry out, as they do; and far more surely than "Mother" would run to hush and comfort her little ones, will our blessed Lord hasten at our call to deliver us from our fears, and from "the power of darkness."[9]

"Ah—but!" you say, "Jesus was not come to them." No, but He was coming; and His presence, whether in darkness or in daylight, is

---

you.

[9] Colossians 1:12-13: *Giving thanks unto the Father, which hath made us meet to be partakers of the inheritance of the saints in light: Who hath delivered us from the power of darkness, and hath translated us into the kingdom of his dear Son.*

all the blessedness we crave.

"It was now dark." Another sort of darkness is that which we voluntarily make for ourselves by willful blindness. We shut our eyes, and cover our heads, and then mourn because we can see no light! We ignorantly, or obstinately, hide ourselves in the shadows, when God's noontide of love and pity is all around us. Oh, that I could so write as to entice some poor soul to open its eyes of faith to the sunshine!

I know, by sad experience, just what you suffer, and how the darkness (from whatever cause) drags you down, and crushes you. You do not utterly distrust your Lord, or disbelieve His Word; but there is a change come over you, and you cannot tell why, or what it is. The days of song and gladness are left behind, and you seem to live now almost without feeling; you pray—as a matter of course—but there is no real drawing near to God in it, no fellowship, for *Jesus does not come to you*. You go about your daily duties, and your work for Christ, in a languid,[10] constrained sort of way, which brings no blessing to yourself or to others. It is sometimes a question with you whether you are spiritually alive at all,

---

[10] Weak, sluggish, weary

whether you have been mistaken all along, and are nothing but a shameful hypocrite. And the very saddest and worst part of it all is, that you are almost content to go on in this sunless, sleepy, sinful way, and "let things take their chance!"[11]

Ah! this is darkness indeed, a wicked darkness, from which you must fly with winged feet. God forbid that you should linger in it another moment, for it is the darkness of the shadow of death; and the longer you remain in it, the blacker will be the gathering night around you. Fly for your life; Jesus is waiting to pardon and restore you. Even as you read these words, the command comes to you, *"Awake, thou that sleepest, and arise from the dead, and Christ shall give thee light."*[12]

---

[11] "Let it run its course," or work out naturally
[12] Ephesians 5:14: *Wherefore he saith, Awake thou that sleepest, and arise from the dead, and Christ shall give thee light.*

A Perilous Pathway

"Lord, bid me come unto Thee on the water."
Matthew 14:28

Poor Peter! What a weary anxious night of toil and watching he had spent in that storm-tossed ship, with a contrary wind blowing hard, and without the presence of his beloved Lord! But now the fourth watch[1] has begun, the day is breaking, and with the first streaks of dawn, hope springs up in his heart that deliverance will come. It comes in a very unexpected manner, as do most of our great mercies. We fear as we enter into the cloud; but, as it envelopes us, we find it luminous with God's gracious manifestion[2] of Himself. These poor disciples "cried out for fear,"[3] when they first saw Jesus, though they had been longing and praying for Him all the night, and should have been prepared for any revelation of His glory. But Peter—loving, impetuous[4]

---

[1] 3 a.m.-6 a.m.
[2] Manifestation-representation, proof, a revealing
[3] Matthew 14:26: *And when the disciples saw him walking on the sea, they were troubled, saying, It is a spirit; and they cried out for fear.*
[4] Hasty, impulsive

Peter—when he heard his Master's voice, was impatient to embrace Him; he could not endure the distance from his Lord which that cruel sea interposed,[5] so he made the great venture that has been an object-lesson of faith to all succeeding generations.

The whole account, as given in the Gospel, is a striking picture of many phases of our Christian life; but in this brief meditation I am looking chiefly at two points on the glowing canvas—permission sought: "Lord, bid me come"; and the perilous pathway: "on the water."

Beloved reader, I will suppose that you, like myself, are longing for the closer realization of Christ's presence, thirsting for nearer and dearer communion with Him, yet, alas! too often failing to obtain an abiding consciousness of it. How are we to secure the blessing? How are we to step out of the old life, into a new and Divine experience? Not by our own efforts, most assuredly. If Peter had essayed[6] to leave his ship without his Lord's command, he would not have planted one foot upon the waves—he would have sunk immediately.

---

[5] To place something between

[6] Tried, attempted

Our dependence upon God is absolute. Our own struggles after likeness to Christ, and fellowship with Him, are, in themselves, unavailing.[7] He must "draw,"[8] or we cannot "run after Him."[9] He must "bid," or we cannot "come."[10] Pride and self-sufficiency are laid in the dust by this doctrine; but that only proves its truth and necessity. And the true believer is impelled[11] by it, not to relinquish his desires, but to increase his earnest pleadings that God would speak the word of sovereign grace.

"Bid me come." Frances Ridley Havergal[12] used to say, "All God's biddings are enablings," and herein lies the secret of the life of faith, that the obedient heart agrees completely with the Lord's declaration, "Without Me ye can do nothing."[13] Ah! dear souls, be very sure that, if

---

[7] Useless, worthless

[8] John 6:44: *No man can come to me, except the Father which hath sent me draw him: and I will raise him up at the last day.*

[9] John 12:19: *The Pharisees therefore said among themselves, Perceive ye how ye prevail nothing? behold, the world is gone after him.* Psalm 63:8: *My soul followeth hard after thee: thy right hand upholdeth me.*

[10] Matthew 14:28: *And Peter answered him and said, Lord, if it be thou, bid me come unto thee on the water.*

[11] Urged, required

[12] Frances Ridley Havergal (1836-1879), English hymn writer. "Take my Life and Let It Be" and "Like a River Glorious" are two of her well-known hymns.

[13] John 15:5: *I am the vine, ye are the branches: He that*

you have a real desire to come to Christ, He gave it to you, and is more than ready to bestow also the power to take that step of faith, "out of self, into Him,"[14] which has hitherto seemed impossible. He is waiting to "bid" you; it is for this that He has come walking over the sea of separation, and so far revealed Himself to you as to make you long to know more of Him; and, as soon as you have learned your own helplessness, and His Almighty strength, quicker than on the wings of the wind will the sweet call reach you, "COME."[15]

"On the water." Now is the test of faith. To walk on the water, was Peter's own proposition; and the Lord granted his request. He could have been at His disciple's side in a moment, and spared him the trial of faith, and the discovery of its feebleness which this experience gave him. But it seems to be the law of the Kingdom, that we come to Christ on the very waves which separate us from Him; and this is doubtless for our profit, that we may

---

abideth in me, and I in him, the same bringeth forth much fruit: for without me ye can do nothing.

[14] Ephesians 4:24: *And that ye put on the new man, which after God is created in righteousness and true holiness.*

[15] Matthew 14:29: *And he said, Come. And when Peter was come down out of the ship, he walked on the water, to go to Jesus.*

again prove our own weakness, and learn to trust wholly in His strength.[16] Perhaps, in the first flush of joy that the Lord has bidden us come, it seems an easy thing to "walk on the water to go to Jesus"; and self-confidence whispers that we are quite able of ourselves to tread the wondrous pathway. But we soon discover our helplessness apart from Him. The wind is boisterous, the waves are threatening, we remember the great deep beneath us, fear overcomes faith, and "beginning to sink," we cry, "Lord, save me!"[17]

Yet how often is it "on the water" that we find a royal road to His dear feet, and how frequently do our fears and infirmities force upon us the conviction that our blessed Master is truly a Divine and Almighty Savior! How quickly His outstretched hand delivers and supports us, how calm and safe we feel when we joyfully realize His immediate presence!

I think the dear Lord must have kept Peter's hand in His own as they walked back to

---

[16] II Corinthians 12:9: *And he said unto me, My grace is sufficient for thee: for my strength is made perfect in weakness. Most gladly therefore will I rather glory in my infirmities, that the power of Christ may rest upon me.*
[17] Matthew 14:30: *But when he saw the wind boisterous, he was afraid; and beginning to sink, he cried, saying, Lord, save me.*

the ship, for the wind did not cease till they were on board; yet we hear of no further fears of sinking. Anyway, I know that, whatever may be the depth or danger of the seas of sin, or sorrow, or trial over which Christ bids us come to Him, His right hand will hold us safely till we reach the fair haven of Emmanuel's Land.

With Jesus, Yet Afraid

"Where is your faith?" Luke 8:25

It was a matter of life or death with these men! To their dim human vision, there were gathered around that little ship, the materials for an awful tragedy! Fierce gusts of stormy wind—devouring waves of the sea—a frail boat every moment in jeopardy of foundering,[1] paralyzing terror in the hearts of all but one of their number—and He was asleep! One can imagine the despair and intensity of the cry with which they awoke Him, "Master! Master! we perish!"[2]

"Then He arose, and rebuked the wind and the raging of the water: and they ceased, and there was a calm." In an instant, the turmoil was over, and the danger gone; but we can imagine the grieved look of reproval[3] in the Lord's face as He turns from the cowering elements, to ask the trembling men at His side

---

[1] Sinking

[2] Luke 8:24: *And they came to him, and awoke him, saying, Master, master, we perish. Then he arose, and rebuked the wind and the raging of the water: and they ceased, and there was a calm.*

[3] To reprove, rebuke, disapprove

the question, "Where is your faith?"[4] "Have the winds scattered it? Has the sea swallowed it up? Has your fear utterly swept it away?"

To us, looking back over the centuries at this incident on the Sea of Galilee, it seems incomprehensible[5] that the disciples could be afraid of anything, while Jesus was with them. We should have thought that His personal presence, whether sleeping or waking, would have been a perfect security to them against all fear of ill. Had they not seen daily manifestations of His mighty power? Had He not healed the sick—opened blind eyes—made lame men walk—multiplied a few loaves and fishes to provide food for a great host[6]—raised the dead to life, and done many other wonderful works? After all they had seen, and felt, and known of His mighty power in the past, one wonders that the present danger should so utterly affright them. The reason of this may have been that they did not go to Jesus at once, as soon as the gale burst upon them. Perhaps they thought that they could

---

[4] Luke 8:25: *And he said unto them, Where is your faith? And they being afraid wondered, saying one to another, What manner of man is this! For he commandeth even the winds and water, and they obey him*

[5] Hard to understand

[6] Multitude, crowd

manage the boat and weather the storm by their own efforts and skill.

It is possible that self-confidence was lurking in their hearts, and that the Lord used this perilous position to convince them of their absolute helplessness and dependence on Himself for everything.

Ah! dear friends, does not this teaching come home to our own hearts? Do not we behave in precisely similar fashion when placed in the same alarming circumstances? Some great trial or temptation bursts like a tempest into the serenity of our life, and overwhelms us with a sense of danger and distress; we are terrified and trembling, we see nothing but the peril which surrounds us, we struggle against the storm as best we can till there is no more endurance in us, and then we go to the Master with the bitter cry of those about to perish!

Yet, as a matter of fact, He has been with us all the time!

Has He not promised never to leave us?[7] Is there not always access by faith to His gracious

---

[7] John 14:18: *I will not leave you comfortless: I will come to you.* Hebrews 13:5: *Let your conversation be without covetousness; and be content with such things as ye have: for he hath said, I will never leave thee, nor forsake thee.*

presence? He may be in the hinder part of the ship, asleep, and apparently oblivious of all that is passing around Him; but the pillow beneath His head is His own Omniscience,[8] and, as surely as He ruled those winds and waves on Galilee's lake, and reined in the tempest with a word, so certainly does He manage all the affairs of His children, and appoint or permit all that concerns them. A sincere and steadfast faith in this blessed fact would keep our minds in perfect peace,[9] whatever might befall us; it would lift us above all fear of the perils and storms of life, and hide us as in "the secret of His tabernacle."[10]

Dear Master, You come to each one of us with the same question as that which shamed Your poor timid disciples, "Where is your faith?" And we are dumb[11] before You, Lord, as they were, for we have no excuse to offer for our unbelief; we have not even the slight plea which they might have urged, that they had as yet scarcely realized that You were God

---

[8] All-knowing

[9] Isaiah 26:3: *Thou wilt keep him in perfect peace, whose mind is stayed on thee: because he trusteth in thee.*

[10] Psalm 27:5: *For in the time of trouble he shall hide me in his pavilion: in the secret of his tabernacle shall he hide me; he shall set me up upon a rock.*

[11] Unable to speak

incarnate, and had asked, wondering among themselves, "What kind of man is this?"[12] We know You as the once crucified, but now risen Lord, to whom all power in Heaven and on earth has been given,[13] and You may well marvel at our unbelief.

Strange indeed it is, that the love of Christ, so boundless and so infinite, should be so grudgingly trusted in by those whose only hope lies in the fullness and freeness of that love as manifested to them. We do not find it difficult to believe and rejoice in the love of a fellow-creature; but when the fathomless[14] love of God is declared to us, we question, and reason, and evade, and calculate, with a stubbornness which only too plainly shows the hardness and unbelief of our heart.

O beloved, let us cast away from us, with shame and loathing, the bonds of this cruel sin of doubting, which grieves our Savior's tender heart, and so shamefully dishonors His love! His pathetic[15] question, "Where is your faith?"

_____

[12] Matthew 8:27: *But the men marveled, saying, What manner of man is this, that even the winds and the sea obey him!*

[13] Matthew 28:18: *And Jesus came and spake unto them, saying, All power is given unto me in heaven and in earth.*

[14] Cannot be understood, cannot be measured

[15] Sad

plainly shows that He expects our absolute trust at all times, and that He is disappointed when He fails to find the faith He so much values in His chosen.

A Sight for Men and Angels

"He shewed them His hands and His feet."
Luke 24:40

Dear Lord, how can I find words sacred and tender enough, to express the thoughts which You have put into my heart? Oh, do help me, that I may tell only that which I have heard, and seen, and my hands have handled, of the Word of Life! Lay Your hand upon mine, as I hold the pen, that it may write only at Your bidding, and by Your authority, for I tremble at the task before me!

It is nearly midnight, and I see a small upper chamber, crowded with anxious and sorrowful people. Two of their number have just come in from a distant village, and they have a wondrous tale to tell of having seen and talked with the blessed Master, whose shameful death by crucifixion—now three days ago—had filled all their hearts with anguish and fear. They had expected such a different ending to that marvelous life! But what can this news mean? Can He have risen from the dead? Their souls are stirred within them as the possibility of this fact dawns upon them. One and another remember that, while He was with them, He spoke of seeing them again; and the two just arrived from Emmaus affirm constantly that they have been in His company, their hearts burning within them as He spoke, and that He "broke bread" with them at the evening meal, thus revealing Himself to them.

Suddenly, while they are questioning and debating, Jesus Himself is in their midst! At once, every voice is hushed, and every heart beats fast with fear, as they scarcely dare to recognize, in this majestic Presence before them, a wondrous likeness to the bruised and wounded human form so lately laid in the grave. Then He speaks—addressing to them the usual salutation of the East, "Peace be with you!" But, at the sound of His voice, a panic of awe seizes them; they are "terrified and affrighted," supposing they see a spirit. Tenderly He calms and soothes them with gentle, reassuring words, and then—as if He were impatient for their welcoming love—"He showed them His hands and His feet."

Blessed Master, that must have been the most marvelous sight that men or angels ever looked upon! The Creator of all worlds standing as a sacrifice for sin before His own fallen creatures! "God manifest in the flesh,"[1] laying bare the wounds which expiated[2] their transgressions! It passes comprehension![3] Lord, enlighten my understanding, that I may know something of this mighty mystery of incarnate[4] love!

"He showed them." Oh, the sweet compassion of Your action, Lord Jesus, the unspeakable love of Your heart, when You did spread out Your pierced hands, and draw aside the robe from Your scarred feet, that the poor, unbelieving, frightened disciples might see the nail-prints, and seeing, might believe, and be at peace! For, were not these wounds of Yours, O Lord, the blessed tokens of Your victory over sin and death; and in thus showing them, did You not, as a Conqueror, gloriously triumph over all Your own and Your people's enemies?

My soul, has your Savior showed to you also, these indelible[5] seals of His dying love for

_____

[1] I Timothy 3:16: *And without controversy great is the mystery of godliness: God was manifest in the flesh, justified in the Spirit, seen of angels, preached unto the Gentiles, believed on in the world, received up into glory.*

[2] Atoned for, paid for

[3] To understand

[4] To take on human form

[5] Permanent

you? And, beholding them, have you realized the enormity of your guiltiness in God's sight, which could be pardoned only at such a price as this? Can you not hear Him say, "I suffered this for you"—and can you, unmoved, see such a sight, and hear such words? Nay, rather must your full heart follow the experience of those disciples to whom the amazing revelation was first made, for it is recorded that "they believed not for joy, and wondered."[6]

"His hands and His feet." Those hands which had done so many sweet deeds of mercy, those feet which had made so many weary journeys to help, and bless, and save others are now bearing the marks of the cruel suffering endured for my sake. Lord Jesus, my heart melts with love and grief, as I ponder on the unknown agonies of Your atonement! For these scars on Your hands, and Your feet, and Your side are but the outer physical tokens of the inner spiritual anguish, bruising, and smiting of Your soul for my sin!

O Heavenly Love, my faith sees You as You did stand that night in the veiled majesty of Your resurrection life, pleading, by the

---

[6] Luke 24:41: *And while they yet believed not for joy, and wondered, he said unto them, Have ye here any meat?*

eloquence of those "poor dumb mouths"[7] on Your sacred body, that those whom You Had loved "even unto death"[8] should believe in You, and trust You for their soul's salvation!

My soul, come afresh to your risen Lord, this morning, and ask Him to show you again something of what His love for you cost Him! Your pardon is in His passion,[9] your healing in His stripes, your life in His death!

The two Marys "came and held Him by the feet, and worshiped Him."[10] Do this also; and while, with penitent love and fully-surrendered heart, you adore Him, He will accept you, and give you grace to say, "My Lord, and my God!"[11]

---

[7] Scars of the nails in His hands and feet and the wound in His side

[8] Philippians 2:8: *And being found in fashion as a man, he humbled himself, and became obedient unto death, even the death of the cross.*

[9] His crucifixion

[10] Matthew 28:9: *And as they went to tell his disciples, behold, Jesus met them, saying, All hail. And they came and held him by the feet, and worshipped him.*

[11] John 20:28: *And Thomas answered and said unto him, My Lord and my God.*

An Unchangeable God

"Jesus Christ the same yesterday, and today, and forever." Hebrews 13:8

An Unchangeable God! O heart of mine, inconstant[1] and wavering, is not the fact that you have an immutable[2] God, one of your choicest comforts; is it not the blessed sanctuary where alone your weary wings can fold themselves to perfect rest? When friends fail and forsake, when earthly joys vanish, when a sense of the instability[3] of the world's firmest things shakes your whole being with a great dread, and your own fickleness[4] is the saddest part of it all—then, your Lord's immutability[5] is a tower of refuge[6], into which you can enter, and cling fearlessly to His assurance, "I am the Lord, I change not."[7]

---

[1] Changeable

[2] Unchangeable, unchanging

[3] Shakiness, uncertainty, insecurity, unsteadiness

[4] Inconsistent, flighty, changeable

[5] Never changing

[6] Psalm 18:2: *The LORD is my rock, and my fortress, and my deliverer; my God, my strength, in whom I will trust; my buckler, and the horn of my salvation, and my high tower.*

[7] Malachi 3:6: *For I am the LORD, I change not; therefore ye sons of Jacob are not consumed.*

If the Spirit of God will open to us the door of our text, we shall at once have entrance into the heavenly places in Christ Jesus. At the very threshold, His Name is as sweet-dropping myrrh; and on the door-posts and lintel, we see the dark and sacred stains which tell the wondrous story of salvation through His sacrifice, and life by His death.[8] If we do but begin to speak of Jesus Christ—of "His great love wherewith He loved us,"[9] and His atoning death for us—we are quickly ushered into "the secret place of the Most High," where we may "abide under the shadow of the Almighty."[10] Blessed Name! It is the master-key to all Heaven's portals, the "open sesame" of the gates of Paradise.

"Jesus Christ—the same." Think of the never-varying purpose of our Savior's existence, both human and Divine. As He was in eternity, covenanting with His Father to bear our sins, and to impute[11] to us His

---

[8] Exodus 12:1-13, the Passover

[9] Ephesians 2:4-5: *But God, who is rich in mercy, for his great love wherewith he loved us, Even when we were dead in sins, hath quickened us together with Christ, (by grace ye are saved;)*

[10] Psalm 91:1: *He that dwelleth in the secret place of the most High shall abide under the shadow of the Almighty.*

[11] To credit, assign

righteousness; as He was on earth, loving—blessing—healing—pitying—saving; as He was in life, in death, in resurrection, and in ascension—"this same Jesus"[12] is now, and ever will be. He has never changed; His tenderness has never varied; His compassions have never failed. May He enable us to realize the eternal repose and fixedness of His designs of love and mercy, that we may trust Him as unreservedly as such a God deserves to be trusted!

"Yesterday." The Lord of all Creation knows not the boundaries of time. The Scripture says, "A thousand years in Your sight are but as yesterday when it is past, and as a watch in the night."[13] Then, to Him it is but as yesterday, since He gave His life to ransom our souls! How He must have loved us—was it not "even unto death?" His heart was filled with such tender pity for us, as poor lost sinners, that He endured the cross, He bore the awful weight of God's wrath, that pardon and acceptance might be possible for us—and He

---

[12] Acts 1:11: *Which also said, Ye men of Galilee, why stand ye gazing up into heaven? this same Jesus, which is taken up from you into heaven, shall so come in like manner as ye have seen him go into heaven.*

[13] Psalm 90:4: *For a thousand years in thy sight are but as yesterday when it is past, and as a watch in the night.*

loves us now with just that very same love which yesterday caused Him to die! Does not this thought move our hearts to peace and joy in believing? Can we not rest our burdened souls on such a steadfast Savior?

"Today." He is on His Throne today, reigning and ruling, with all power in Heaven, and earth, and hell; but He is still "this same Jesus." He wears His priesthood still, and is pleading for His people, calling them to follow Him, cleansing them, opening their blind eyes, and delivering them from death. We sometimes think that, if we could but see the Lord Jesus, and fall at His feet, and touch the hem of His garment,[14] and sob out all our griefs in His lovely presence, we should then have the full assurance of faith, and never, never doubt Him again. Ah! but that would be sight, not faith; and this could not glorify Him as our perfect trust can do. "In whom, though now ye see Him not, yet believing, ye rejoice with joy unspeakable and full of glory."[15]

"And forever." Dear reader, what has Jesus

---

[14] Matthew 9:21: *For she said within herself, If I may but touch his garment, I shall be whole.*

[15] I Peter 1:8-9: *Whom having not seen, ye love; in whom, though now ye see him not, yet believing, ye rejoice with joy unspeakable and full of glory: Receiving the end of your faith, even the salvation of your souls.*

Christ been to you in the past years? Have you any fault to find with Him? Has He not loved, and pardoned, and blessed, and borne with you as only such a gracious Lord could do? What is He to you today? Does not your helpless soul still hang on Him? Have you any other plea than His most precious blood—any hope but in His merit? Has He ever cast you from Him, and refused the mercy you have asked?

"Ah, no!" you say, "'He is all my salvation, and all my desire'[16] and though I have treated no other friend so ill, I have proved that, 'As the Heaven is high above the earth, so great is His mercy toward those who fear Him.'"[17]

Then, let the past assure you for the future. All He has been to you, all He now is, He will still be, not only tomorrow, but "forever."

"Unchangeable His will,
Whatever be my frame;

---

[16] II Samuel 23:5: *Although my house be not so with God; yet he hath made with me an everlasting covenant, ordered in all things, and sure: for this is all my salvation, and all my desire, although he make it not to grow.*

[17] Psalm 103:11-12: *For as the heaven is high above the earth, so great is his mercy toward them that fear him. As far as the east is from the west, so far hath he removed our transgressions from us.*

His loving heart is still
Eternally the same:
My soul through many changes goes,
His love, no variation knows."[18]

---

[18] William Hammond (1719-1783), English hymn writer

About the Editor

Dr. Teresa Suttles is a Christian educator and author. She holds graduate degrees in Christian Education and in Classical Studies.

She and her husband John, pastor of Coweta Particular Baptist Church, have four married children and ten grandchildren.

Other Books by the Editor

The Little Gray Box

John Bunyan's The Holy War: An Updated Edition

Christian Biography Series

The Life of John Bunyan

Thongzai Mamma: The Life of Marilla Baker Ingalls

Under the Hopia Tree: The Life of Ann Judson

Gentle and Quiet Strength: 6 Ladies, 5 Brilliant Hymnwriters

The Mighty Side of Weaker

Mrs. Spurgeon Books Edited by this Author

A Basket of Summer Fruit

A Cluster of Camphire

A Carillon of Bells

www.cowetaparticularbaptist.org

Manufactured by Amazon.ca
Bolton, ON

31320779R00068